AGILE SOFTWARE DEVELOPMENT IN THE LARGE

Also Available from Dorset House Publishing

Adaptive Software Development: A Collaborative Approach to Managing Complex Systems
by James A. Highsmith III   foreword by Ken Orr
ISBN: 0-932633-40-4   Copyright ©2000   392 pages, softcover

The Deadline: A Novel About Project Management
by Tom DeMarco
ISBN: 0-932633-39-0   Copyright ©1997   320 pages, softcover

Endgame: Mastering the Final Stage of Software Development
by Robert Galen
ISBN: 0-932633-62-5   Copyright ©2004   288 pages, softcover

Five Core Metrics: The Intelligence Behind Successful Software Management
by Lawrence H. Putnam and Ware Myers
ISBN: 0-932633-55-2   Copyright ©2003   328 pages, softcover

Hiring Technical People: The Artful Science of Getting the Right Person for the Job
by Johanna Rothman   foreword by Gerald M. Weinberg
ISBN: 0-932633-59-5   Copyright ©2004   416 pages, softcover

Peopleware: Productive Projects and Teams, 2nd ed.
by Tom DeMarco and Timothy Lister
ISBN: 0-932633-43-9   Copyright ©1999   264 pages, softcover

Project Retrospectives: A Handbook for Team Reviews
by Norman L. Kerth   foreword by Gerald M. Weinberg
ISBN: 0-932633-44-7   Copyright ©2001   288 pages, softcover

Slack: Getting Past Burnout, Busywork, and the Myth of Total Efficiency
by Tom DeMarco
ISBN: 0-932633-61-7   Copyright ©2001   240 pages, hardcover

Waltzing with Bears: Managing Risk on Software Projects
by Tom DeMarco and Timothy Lister
ISBN: 0-932633-60-9   Copyright ©2003   208 pages, softcover

For More Information

✔ Contact us for prices, shipping options, availability, and more.

✔ Sign up for *DHQ: The Dorset House Quarterly* in print or PDF.

✔ Send e-mail to subscribe to *e-DHQ*, our e-mail newsletter.

✔ Visit Dorsethouse.com for excerpts, reviews, downloads, and more.

DORSET HOUSE PUBLISHING
An Independent Publisher of Books on
Systems and Software Development and Management. Since 1984.
353 West 12th Street   New York, NY 10014   USA
1-800-DH-BOOKS   1-800-342-6657
212-620-4053   fax: 212-727-1044
info@dorsethouse.com   www.dorsethouse.com

AGILE SOFTWARE DEVELOPMENT IN THE LARGE

Diving Into the Deep

Jutta Eckstein

DORSET HOUSE PUBLISHING
353 WEST 12TH STREET
NEW YORK, NEW YORK 10014

Library of Congress Cataloging-in-Publication Data

Eckstein, Jutta.
    Agile software development in the large : diving into the deep / Jutta Eckstein.
        p. cm.
    Includes bibliographical references and index.
    ISBN 0-932633-57-9
    1.   Computer software--Development. I. Title.
    QA76.76.D47E28 2004
    005.3--dc22

                                                    2004010164

Front Cover Photograph: Stefan Krahe
Cover Design & Interior Illustrations: Katja Gloggengiesser, www.gloggengiesser.com

Copyright © 2004 by Jutta Eckstein. Published by Dorset House Publishing, 353 West 12th Street, New York, NY 10014.

Distributed in the English language in Singapore, the Philippines, and Southeast Asia by Alkem Company (S) Pte. Ltd., Singapore; in the English language in India, Bangladesh, Sri Lanka, Nepal, and Mauritius by Prism Books Pvt., Ltd., Bangalore, India; and in the English language in Japan by Toppan Co., Ltd., Tokyo, Japan.

Printed in the United States of America

Library of Congress Catalog Number: 2004010164

ISBN: 0-932633-57-9   12   11   10   9   8   7   6   5   4   3   2   1

ACKNOWLEDGMENTS

A mountain is not in the need of a mountain,
But the human is in the need of a human.
      —Basque proverb

A book like this is always the result of many years of development. That's why it is so difficult to thank all the people who supported its creation. I would like to apologize in advance to all those people I may have accidentally forgotten.

First, though, I would like to thank Frank Westphal, who suggested that I accompany him to a remote island to concentrate on writing (Frank was writing his book on test-driven development). My sister, Eva Eckstein—a librarian—gave us the idea of hiding on the island of Hiddensee in the Baltic Sea, where many German writers—including several winners of the Nobel Prize in Literature (Thomas Mann, Gerhard Hauptmann, Günter Grass, among others)—created their marvelous works. Thus, we sat on Hiddensee and waited for the same thing to happen to us that happened to one of Günter Grass's protagonists.[1]

> As soon as he arrived at Hiddensee, he got the irresistible urge to . . . write.

---

[1] Günter Grass, *Ein weites Feld* (Göttingen, Germany: Steidl Verlag, 1995), p. 333.

And, in fact, it worked! However, once most of the text was written, I needed the help of many other people to finally make a book out of it.

First, I would like to thank my family. Preceding all others is my partner, Nicolai M. Josuttis, who gave his moral support as well as his thoughts in uncountable discussions that helped shape the book into what you have in your hands right now. Next, my cousin Katja Gloggengiesser, whose illustrations give the book that personal touch. Finally, someone I consider a member of my family, my long-time flatmate Monika Bobzien, for the endless discussions on our balcony. Again and again, she flagged me down to broaden my horizons.

Furthermore, I would like to thank the following:

The authors of the expert boxes, who enriched the book with their personal experiences: Alistair Cockburn, David Hussman, Diana Larsen, Dierk König, Joshua Kerievsky, Nicolai M. Josuttis, and Stefan Roock. All the reviewers, who helped to shape the book with their comments, some brief and some extensive: Daniel Schweizer, Dave Thomas from Pragmatic Programmers, Dierk König, Eberhard Wolff, Frank Maurer (who wasn't afraid to use the very first draft of the book as course material at the University of Toronto), James Noble, Jon Kern, Ken Schwaber, Martin Müller-Rohde, Mike Cohn, Robert Wenner, Stefan Roock, and Vanita Shroff.

Jens Coldewey, whose wonderful birthday present helped me to find the appropriate introductory quotes and proverbs for the individual chapters.

Stefan Krahe, one of my dive instructors, who took the magnificent picture of the Indian mackerels for the front cover.

And not least, a special thank you to the team at Dorset House: I would like to point out Vincent Au, who made the book readable, and David McClintock, for his belief in the project right from the beginning.

Finally, I would like to thank all of those who accompanied me on my journey through different projects, conferences, training, and workshops, and who shared with me the experience of learning.

CONTENTS

PREFACE

A book is always a prevented dialogue.
—Hans Urs von Balthasar

Looking back on all my years in software development, I discover something extraordinary: Besides the technological progress, revolutions, and unfulfilled promises, the occupational image has changed. In the past, I was a software developer, solving local technical problems. Now, my job is to make sure that the outcome of a whole software project makes sense. The reason for this change is that too many projects are failing, and this failure isn't caused by technology, but by social, structural, and organizational deficits.

It is all made worse by tool providers who promise heaven and earth, by clients who create the illusion of unrealistic schedules, and by market pressure that loads significant risks on every large project.

However, when I compare the projects I'm working on, only trivialities come to mind. But those trivialities actually hold the key to project success: Instead of making inappropriate decisions, I place value in common sense and create an environment that enables constructive communication.

However, the times are changing. It is just not possible anymore to finance failed large projects. Those who want to stay in business have to deliver fast and timely solutions. Agile processes help developers concentrate on the essentials. Unfortunately, there are only a few real-life examples of how agile processes can support large projects.

This book is intended to close that gap, drawing on the essence of my experience in large agile projects. The book mirrors my discovery that the social aspects of development always outweigh the technical ones. This is why I sometimes call myself a communication manager (although my technical background has proven necessary for being taken seriously not only by management but also by developers).

I hope you have fun reading the book. I invite you to visit the book at my Website, http://www.jeckstein.com/agilebook, and to contact me at agilebook@jeckstein.com.

April 2004   J.E.
Munich, Germany

AGILE SOFTWARE DEVELOPMENT IN THE LARGE

1

INTRODUCTION

Big stone is hard to throw.
    —German proverb

Imagine you have to develop an application that will support traders in the front office of a financial institution. The traders have to be able to buy and sell products and calculate the risk of each transaction. One major difficulty is that the products available for trading are constantly changing. If you focus on the options market, you will see that almost every other day, a new product (option) is available for trade, traded differently than the others, and whose underlying risk must also be treated differently. Therefore, if you ask your client for the system requirements today, you will probably get a different answer than if you were to ask her tomorrow. Furthermore, she will let you know that without the application, she is unable to trade these new options. With each day that passes without her being able to use your application, her company loses several hundred thousand dollars. As if that weren't bad enough, she also points out that the competition is already able to trade these options. She assures you that any kind of support your application can provide for these products would help to reduce the loss, because she can perform some of the steps manually. So she does not insist on having full trading support for the new products, although it would definitely be a plus.

A similar situation could occur in the telecommunications sector, or in any domain with a focus on e-business. The big difference between these more modern applications and more traditional applications is that the modern ones must be available in the market quickly. Otherwise, the application could already be obsolete by the time it is first used, or the company might be run out of business. Sometimes, it is more important to serve the customer's *basic* needs *quickly* than to fulfill *all* her requirements *later*, which might end up being too late.

Heavyweight processes of the 1980's and 1990's have difficulties dealing with these new requirements. They have instead occasionally been successful in domains with *stable* requirements. In these domains, everything can be formalized, and a detailed plan can be set up at the very beginning. Furthermore, every project can "blindly" follow this plan without needing to worry about updating or modifying it. Examples of this are defense projects, or projects from the airline or nuclear power plant industries. As well as stable requirements, these projects often seem to have limitless cost and time budgets. Because of this, it is more important to fulfill *all* the requirements than to deliver a subset of them on time and in budget. However, this objective is also changing in these domains. For instance, in the defense sector, processes that support changing requirements are becoming increasingly important.

Agile processes promise to react flexibly to these continuously changing requirements. That is why agile processes are currently treated as a panacea for successful software development. However, agile processes are almost always recommended for small projects and small teams only—bad news for those large teams that have to deal with speedy requirements changes.

That is the reason this book deals with agile processes in large projects. But before we discuss this topic in detail, I would like to further define the focus and target audience of this book. First, it is necessary to explain the terms *large, agile,* and *agile process* and the context in which they are used.

Questioning Scaling Agile Processes

Software engineers tend to question the feasibility of agile software development in the large, not only because most agile processes claim to work mainly for small teams, but also because most of the projects that fail are large. The reason most (large) projects fail is a lack of communication: among teammates, between team and manager, between team and customer, and so on. Communication is one of the focal points of agile processes. But can effective communication ever be established successfully for large teams? The popular opinion is that it can't, leading to the idea that if you have a hundred people on a development team and get rid of all but the top twenty or (preferably) fewer, the chances for project success will rise significantly.

However, you can't generally avoid large projects. Sometimes, you will face constraints that force you to run a large project with a large team. For instance, some projects have such a large scope that it is not possible to realize it with a small team in the defined time frame.

If you want to take advantage of agile processes, several questions arise: Are agile processes able to scale? That is, Can they be amplified in order to support large projects? And, moreover, are they able to support large projects? And what kind of problems occur when an enterprise decides to use an agile process for a large, perhaps even mission-critical, project? This book tries to answer these and many questions relating to agile software development. But, before we go into more detail, I should better clarify what I mean by *large* projects.

Examining Largeness

In my experience, I have found that a project can be considered large in many dimensions. For example, the money, scope, amount of people, and risks involved can be large. These different "dimensions" of largeness are mostly interrelated. Some dimensions exist as a first-order consequence of the requirements and constraints. Others are derived from these first-order dimensions.

The individual dimensions of largeness and their interrelations are defined as follows:

- **Scope** is a first-order dimension of largeness, created by the amount and complexity of the requirements. If a project is large in scope, you can either address that issue by allowing a large time frame, making the project large in the sense of the time it requires. The other possibility would be to allocate a large staff to the project. In this way, the scope dimension influences the time and people dimensions.

- **Time** is rarely considered a first-order dimension in software development. I mean, I have never encountered a company that decided to work on a project over 20 years, just to kill time. Some projects may go on forever, though, because nobody has the courage to cancel them. But time is never the reason for starting a project. It is typically a dimension that follows another dimension. For example, if the risk of the project is high because you have a number of unskilled people on your staff, you will need to have them trained, which will take time.

SKILL RISK.

- **Money** is also typically a second-order dimension. This means high costs are always a consequence of the growths of some other dimensions. At least, I have never seen a project that was started just because there was a lot of spare cash lying around. On the other hand, I have seen a lot of projects waste enormous amounts of money without batting an eye. But this was always a consequence of one of the other dimensions. For example, a large team could cost a lot of money, but the question of whether it is necessary to have such a large team is rarely raised.

- **People** are a different matter. The number of project members is usually a first-order dimension. It is possible for the size of a project's staff to be a side effect of the scope of the project. However, projects are sometimes staffed with a lot of people—in the worst case, right from the beginning—mainly to show the importance of the project, or of the project management. The amount of project members may not only be related to the amount of developers, but also for example to the number of customers. The more customers are involved in the project, the higher the risk of contradictory requirements.

- **Risk** is a much more complicated dimension because it can refer to almost anything. For example, team size can be a risk, but focusing on a hot technology also carries a big risk and is often followed by having to spend money to train

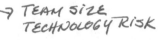

TEAM SIZE
TECHNOLOGY RISK

the staff, among other things. However, risk is typically a second-order dimension.

Therefore, the two initial reasons for scaling a project are scope and people. You can definitely run a large-scope project with a small team. But large-scope projects are almost always developed by a large team—especially in large companies.

Typically, if a project is large in terms of people, all its other dimensions are probably just as large. For example, you will hardly ever find a large team working on a project with a narrow scope, a schedule of only three months, or a budget of only a few hundred thousand dollars. The project itself might not carry any extraordinary risk, but scaling all the project's dimensions implies a risk of its own. For instance, if a lot of money is involved, there is a high risk that a lot of money will be lost. Or, if the time frame is extremely large, the risk that the project will never be finished at all increases.

In this book, I focus on projects with large teams. However, due to the fact that large teams also usually scale the dimensions of scope, time, money, and risk, these other dimensions will not be ignored.

Raising Large Issues

Of course, *large* is not a well-defined magnitude, and neither is the largeness of a team. Will a team be considered large if it contains 2, 10, 100, 1,000, or even more people? And what impact does every additional order of magnitude in staff number have on the process? For example, let's look at its influence on communication:

- **2 people and more:** If a project is developed by only one person, that person should have the big picture of the project in mind. He or she knows the whole system in terms of code and design. As soon as another person is added to the project, these two people will have to communicate with each other. Communication is the only thing that will enable both developers to understand what is going on and to further coordinate their efforts. For example, it would be annoying if they both worked on the same programming task unknowingly, only to find out once they began to integrate the code.

- **10 people or more:** With teams of this size, you have to start coordinating members' efforts and their communication. You have to explicitly establish communication channels in order to discuss topics with the whole group.
- **100 people or more:** Even if you have an open-plan office available, teams of this size will not fit in a single room. Therefore, across the entire team, you have to strategically foster the kind of "natural" communication that would take place inside a single room.
- **1,000 people or more:** Chances are high that this team will not only be distributed over several rooms, but also over several buildings, perhaps over several locations. Consequently, the people on the team are unlikely to know all their teammates.

This example shows not only that large is relative, but also that scaling can lead to different consequences.

Specifying the Projects in Focus

This book is derived from my experience on projects with teams ranging in size from one to two-hundred people. I learned a lot about scaling agile processes while working with these different-sized teams. In my experience, you will encounter significant changes in dynamics with a team of twenty or more. So, although this book deals mainly with issues faced by teams with more than one hundred members, those projects with ten or more people will also benefit from this book, especially if they are embedded in a large organization.

Due to the limits of my own experience, I do not examine the special aspects of teams with 1,000 people or more. However, I assume that issues and challenges similar to those I address in this book are experienced in these circumstances. This book attempts to elucidate the agile value system and show a way to preserve these values on large projects. Doing so clarifies the difference between the agile value system and its realization in a specific process, such as Extreme Programming.

My experience is mainly with co-located teams that outsourced only minor parts of their development effort. Although dispersed development is not a focal topic of this book, I discuss it in Chapters 3 and 6.

The projects I worked on were varied in nature. I worked with teams in the financial sector, the automobile industry, telecommunications, and the software industry.

Of course, I have exchanged my experiences with a lot of other people, most of whom had experiences similar to mine, on teams that were similarly sized. Some of them have experience with teams of 350 people or more and still encountered the sort of challenges I discuss.

In this way, the issues and suggestions pointed out in this book are based on experiences with large teams and large projects—either my own or those of my colleagues.

Detecting the Agile Method for Scaling

This book neither presents agile processes in general, nor does it present any agile methodology in particular. (However, at the beginning of the next chapter, I provide a very brief introduction to the fundamentals of agile processes.[1]) So, although you might, for example, detect some techniques that remind you of Extreme Programming, neither the title nor the focus of this book is *Scaling Extreme Programming*. It is, however, possible to scale some of the practices of Extreme Programming so they are therefore beneficial to large teams. And, in parallel, they support the underlying value system of agile processes.

As we shall discuss later (see Chapter 3), a large team is typically split into many smaller teams. Because a lot has been said already about agile processes in small teams, I do not focus on the processes these subteams are using. Instead, I concentrate on the process that brings them all together and enables them—despite the large number of people—to work together with agility. Therefore, rather than focus on every aspect of agile processes, I concentrate only on those that work differently in large projects developed by large teams.

---

[1] If you are looking for in-depth information about agile processes, I suggest you read Alistair Cockburn's *Agile Software Development* first. See the References for details.

The problem is that processes, including agile processes, do not scale linearly. Depending on the "jump" in size, completely new difficulties may occur. The differences are rooted in the fact that some parts of the process cannot be done well by large teams and require a specific treatment. Other differences are the problems that arise solely in large teams, such as communication, as we have seen before.

Thus, instead of scaling a particular agile method, this book presents best practices that allow us to scale up agile principles by respecting the agile value system.

Identifying the Reader

The book is aimed at *change agents:* the people who want to create and establish an agile process despite the difficulties of doing so on a large team. Change agents on small projects in a non-agile environment will also benefit from the practices presented in some of the chapters—Chapter 6, "Agility and the Company," in particular. I assume that the change agent already has some familiarity with agile processes in general or with a particular process (Extreme Programming, for example). Moreover, this book will definitely be of interest for people who

- have tried and failed to use agile methodologies on large projects
- have succeeded in using agile methodologies on large projects
- have not tried agile methodologies on large projects but would like to do so
- are firm believers of the linear (waterfall) model and think agile processes do not work (especially on large projects)
- are firm believers of agile processes but think they would never work on large projects

So, as a change agent, you are probably working on a large team as a project manager, a process coach, a consultant, or a developer. You would like to use an agile process for the large project you are working on, but are unsure how.

Revealing the Structure of the Book

The book has the following structure:

- Chapter 2, "Agility and Largeness," examines the princi- ples and value system of agile processes, raising the diffi- cult question of how they affect large teams.
- The focus of Chapter 3, "Agility and Large Teams," is the impact on a team of a switch to an agile process. How does it affect the team members, and how can you allocate the roles and create the subteams necessary to make it all work? Also in this chapter, we look at virtual teams, using distributed teams and the open source community as examples.
- Chapter 4, "Agility and the Process," concentrates on the characteristics of the process that will allow you to coordi- nate several subteams without regimenting them. The goal is for all the different teams to pull together by remaining agile in their activities.
- In Chapter 5, "Agility and Technology," we look at how the size of the project and the team influence the underlying architecture. We examine the role of the architectural lead and how the architecture can provide a service for the team. We also discuss some techniques and good practices that help to define an agile system.
- Typically, large projects are run by large companies. And large companies bring their own burden to a project. Chapter 6, "Agility and the Company," deals with the problems a big enterprise loads on an agile project.
- Chapter 7, "Putting It All Together: A Project Report," pre- sents a concrete, coherent experience report on a large agile project.

2

AGILITY AND LARGENESS

Values can only be preserved by change.
—Richard Löwenthal

In the first two sections that follow, we look at the fundamentals of agile processes. If you are already familiar with this topic, you might want to skip to the third section, where we examine how agile principles apply to large projects.

Because agile methodologies are trendy right now and a lot of people claim to follow an agile approach, in this chapter, we describe how to uncover processes that are masquerading as agile processes.

Switching to an agile process requires a change in culture, which we discuss in the section after that. One of the main characteristics of agile processes is their ability to adjust to the needs of the project. It is a good practice to figure out the needs of the project and of the team members through open and honest communication.

When first confronted with an agile process, a person's initial reaction is often skepticism about the applicability of the process. Typically, you will discover that people tend to cite the same reasons why they don't believe agile processes could work. This is the topic of the last section of this chapter.

Fundamentals of Agile Processes

Agile processes promise to react flexibly to changing requirements, thus providing the highest business value to the customer at any point in time. As a result of this, the people performing the process are always in focus. The Agile Manifesto, which we discuss in the next subsection, says that individuals and interactions are more important than processes and tools; they question themselves for the better of the people. But can people still be in the center of a process if they number not a dozen, but one hundred?

The objective of an agile approach is to ensure the early detection and elimination of risks during software development. Partitioning of the system, and the iterative development of these partitions, reduces the complexity of the system. This evolutionary approach creates tangible results early on, providing feedback that allows us to take any necessary corrective actions immediately.

Such an iterative and incremental approach is one of the foundations of all agile processes, allowing us to obtain early warnings about the risks that can occur during development. Only through this early feedback are we enabled to address those risks. However, only short and time-boxed development cycles provide frequent feedback. A time-box implies that the time frame for a development cycle is fixed. If the cycles are not short, it will take too long for the corresponding feedback to be received. If the development cycles are not time-boxed, there is a high risk that they will take longer than intended and that, once again, feedback will be postponed. But time-boxing is not what is important; the development cycle's responsiveness to change carries the most weight, and this, in turn, is simplified by using a time-boxed approach.

Planning an agile development cycle always assumes that the following project parameters are fixed:

- **Time:** The development cycle spans the defined time frame. For example, at the beginning of the project, the length of the development cycle is set at four weeks.
- **Resources:** The development cycle draws on resources. It is not very likely that, during the short time frame of a development cycle, the size of the team will change unexpectedly.

- **Quality:** All results should show the same kind of acceptable quality.

The final project parameter, **scope,** is the only one that is kept variable and can change. The release at the end of a development cycle might attain either more or less functionality than planned. But the cycle ends at the determined time, the required resources are determined in advance, and the end product meets the required standard of quality.

The well-known phases of development—analysis, design, implementation, and testing—also exist in an iterative, incremental process. Yet, in agile development, those phases are not performed sequentially; they are performed in parallel. Therefore, testing cannot be decoupled from implementation, nor design from implementation. So, during coding or testing, you might make some discoveries that directly affect the design of the system. These discoveries enable a permanent flexibility that allows us to improve the design continuously during the whole development process. In the words of consultant and author Jim Highsmith,

> While a workflow approach is appropriate for some things—for example, processing an automobile insurance claim—it does not work for product development. Many product development activities are concurrent, with partial completion and, later, refinement being the norm.[1]

Despite the rapid change and extreme flexibility of agile development, it is still very important to coordinate the different activities. For example, never attempt to improve the system's existing design while implementing a new feature.

Although agile processes are treated as a panacea in a lot of circumstances, they often have to be adapted to the specific needs of the project. A defined agile process has to be regarded as a starting line, which later on has to be adapted. Therefore, the key to effectively establishing an agile process is the adaptability of the process itself. It is not necessary for project members themselves to adapt to the process; rather, the process has to follow the people. There-

---

[1]James A. Highsmith III, "Agile Methodologies: Problems, Principles and Practices" (International Conference on eXtreme Programming and Agile Processes in Software-Engineering 2001, Sardinia, Italy, 2001).

fore, it is important that instead of the process being *adopted*, it should be *adapted*.

Adaptation is based on regular reflections about the process. Typically, these reflections (or retrospectives) have two levels. The first level involves reflecting on the project's status. This helps to address obstacles that hinder progress. The second, or *meta*, level reflects on the current support of the process. On the meta level, everyone on the team helps to shape the process so it serves them as best as possible. Of course, the bigger the team, the harder it is to adapt the process, because more people mean more opinions about the process and more requirements will be formulated for the process. However, there is not a lot of guidance out there on how to establish and adapt an agile process for a large team.

The Agile Manifesto

The Agile Alliance is a federation of different representatives of what were formerly known as lightweight processes.[2] The best-known processes within the Agile Alliance are probably

- Adaptive Software Development[3]
- Crystal Methodologies[4]
- Extreme Programming[5]
- Feature Driven Development[6]
- Scrum[7]

Despite the competitive relationship between the representatives of each lightweight process, members of the Agile Alliance were able to come up with a conclusion in the Manifesto. According to Jim Highsmith, one of the Manifesto's authors, there are no plans to

---

[2]For more information on the Agile Alliance, and to read the Agile Manifesto, see http://www.agilealliance.org/.
[3]For Adaptive Software Development, see http://www.adaptivesd.com/.
[4]For Crystal Methodologies, see http://alistair.cockburn.us/crystal/crystal.html.
[5]For Extreme Programming, see http://c2.com/cgi/wiki?ExtremeProgrammingRoadmap.
[6]For Feature Driven Development, see http://www.featuredrivendevelopment.com/.
[7]For Scrum, see http://www.controlchaos.com/.

develop this conclusion into a unified agile process.[8] Below are the main points of interest in the Manifesto:

- **Individuals and interactions over processes and tools:** In the center of all agile processes is clearly the individual. This means an agile process will never be introduced or established over the heads of the project members. The project members are the ones who determine and fine-tune the agile process.

- **Working software over comprehensive documentation:** The idea is to always work toward the main goal: working, acceptable software. No artifact will be developed for its own sake.

- **Customer collaboration over contract negotiation:** Customer satisfaction is the only valid measurement for whether or not a piece of software is acceptable. Experience has taught me that neither developers nor managers are clairvoyant. Therefore, to achieve the highest possible level of user satisfaction, you have to work very closely with the customer. Unfortunately, the software client encounters the same (if not more) problems as anybody else who commissions someone to produce a product.

  Using an example posed by Ron Jeffries, imagine you want a blue sweater, so you ask your spouse to find one for you.[9] If you have ever been in this or a similar situation, you are probably aware of the problems you will face. Even if you describe your desired sweater down to the very last detail, chances are high that you will not be satisfied with the selection your spouse makes, even if it fulfills all of your requirements. On the other hand, if you decide to look for the sweater yourself, you will probably end up buying a completely different one than you thought you would. This is because the requirements are sharpened based on possible alternatives. In other words, if you send

---

[8]James A. Highsmith III, "Agile Methodologies: Problems, Principles and Practices" (International Conference on eXtreme Programming and Agile Processes in Software-Engineering 2001, Sardinia, Italy, 2001).

[9]Ron Jeffries, "Are We Doing XP? How Can We Know and Does It Matter?" (International Conference on eXtreme Programming and Agile Processes in Software-Engineering 2001, Sardinia, Italy, 2001).

your spouse to the store, he or she looks for exactly what you asked for, while if you go yourself, you may see something you like more and, for example, you end up leaving the store with a red sweater (or with a hat and a pair of shoes) instead of the blue sweater you originally wanted.

The same is true for our users—only after they have seen and used the system are they able to know exactly what kind of system they require. And building software is much more complicated than buying a sweater.

- **Responding to change over following a plan:** An agile team will always welcome change. It makes no sense to get angry at a user's request for change or to complain that the user is stupid and should have known what he or she wanted *before* asking you to build it. We have to accept and make the desired changes and, furthermore, we have to support the user in his or her search for the right decision. Only working software provides the necessary support.

The four statements above define the higher value system of agile processes as defined by the Agile Alliance. However, the idea is not to ignore lower values completely. But when in doubt, the higher values always outweigh the lower ones. Thus, it is not bad to follow a plan or to negotiate a contract, but this should not hinder your response to change or your collaboration with the customer.

Think about the sweater example again. Since we are dealing with a large team running a large project, imagine that instead of asking a single person to find the sweater, you ask a hundred people. But, instead of asking each of them to bring you one sweater, you ask for a single one from the entire group. Imagine how hard it will be for the suppliers of the sweater to form, as a group, a common idea of exactly what kind of sweater you want (especially if they do not work with you to obtain feedback early and often in the sweater-selection process).

Or, think about another scenario, in which a hundred customers are asking for a single sweater and are trying to explain this product to you, the supplier. You will probably get a hundred different descriptions; you will have a hard time figuring out which sweater will serve all your customers the best.

Again, in both scenarios, the only useful process is to look for a sweater that serves the customer's needs as you understood them. Get feedback from the customer and iterate your understanding before you come up with the next selection.

Agile Methods with Respect to Largeness

Most agile processes focus on small teams only. Some even specify that they require small teams to succeed, partially because of the lack of experience with large teams using agile processes. For example, Extreme Programming claims to be successful with a typical team size of about twelve people. Although some say they have used Extreme Programming in a larger setting, this information is not well-documented (yet).

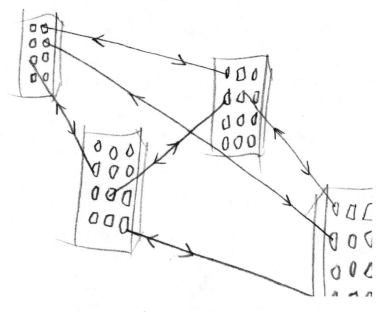

Large teams ...

However, other lightweight methods address larger projects. Two of them seem to be successful—Scrum and Feature Driven Development. Yet, there is not a lot of detailed information available about how these processes really work in large environments.

And last but not least, the Crystal Methodologies acknowledge that the process has to adapt whenever applied to a larger scale. To emphasize this, the Crystal Methodologies define different colors for different scales. For example, Crystal Clear is for teams of up to ten people, and Crystal Orange is for teams of up to forty. Crystal Red, Crystal Blue, and all other darker colors are not specified yet. The Crystal Methodologies recognize the necessity of scaling agile processes, but suggest none for large teams, yet.

Magnifying the Agile Principles

The Agile Manifesto is based on a set of underlying principles. I would like to take a moment to look critically at these principles with respect to their application on projects with large teams:

- **Satisfy the customer through early and continuous delivery of valuable software:** The effort of bringing something into production is often so high that large teams tend to deliver only once. Often, bureaucracy is the main reason for the high level of effort.
- **Welcome changing requirements, even late in development:** Often, you will find that large teams have a complex requirements management process installed, which discourages everybody from requesting changes to requirements. Furthermore, larger teams, especially in large companies, often believe in upfront requirements engineering because people imagine that accepting requirements later will be more expensive than accepting them earlier. Another reason is that people buy into the possibility of clairvoyant engineering, which could eliminate the need to change requirements later.
- **Deliver working software frequently:** Integrating a system with a large team is often regarded as a difficult task. Therefore, you will often find that large teams lean toward developing several subsystems instead of one integrated, working system.
- **Business people and developers work together:** Large companies are often inclined to follow defined communication structures. These structures typically do not respect

19

developers as the peers of business people. So, instead of software people dealing with the customers, another department, such as marketing, often has this task.

- **Trust motivated individuals:** Trust is hardly a characteristic that large organizations are built upon. To compensate for this, large companies are typically structured departmentally, which eases management's control of its employees.

- **Face-to-face conversation:** The size of large teams often hinders members' ability to converse face-to-face. This is why you often find a culture of indirect communication in large teams. But face-to-face communication is one of the most important tools for building trust.

- **Working software is the primary measure of progress:** Although most people would support the truth of this statement, they would act differently. Especially on large projects, you will find that people are often busy developing all kinds of artifacts, most of which are barely related to the development of working software, and are focused instead on documenting different concepts.

- **Promote sustainable development:** This principle is probably the goal for all teams, large or small. Software development can be better compared with a marathon than with a sprint. It is more important to achieve enduring, substantial improvements than to reach the target fast (by, for example, asking the team members to work overtime). However, in large teams, you are likely to find this principle much more difficult to uphold, because of the wide variety of interests and skills of the individual team members.

- **Continuous attention to technical excellence and good design:** The departmental structure of many large organizations sometimes leads to linear development. In other words, certain departments—quality control or design, for example—only appear in the development cycle at specific points in time. Thus, design is often only a topic at the beginning of the project, whereas testing is mainly a topic at the end. This separation tends to result in individuals taking responsibility solely for their own tasks and not regarding themselves as responsible for the success of the whole project. For example, a designer may feel responsible only for the design, and not, for example, the tests. However, only by bringing all these different issues together can the team grow in skill, which will in turn allow the system to improve.

- **Simplicity is essential:** A typical characteristic of large teams is that they tend to define a framework first, without respecting the skills and the size of the team, even without respecting the concrete requirements. Developing a framework first puts too much focus on generalization, which in turn leads to an architecture that is more complex than required.

- **Self-organizing teams:** People often assume that a large team can't be self-organized and, to compensate, they put a controlling hierarchy in place. Yet control is often understood as a sign of mistrust, which often has negative effects on team morale.

But who is the LEADER

- **Team reflection and adjustment:** Under the cloak of support, large companies tend to define a development process that should be used for all kinds of project development. I have never seen a company that encourages teams to define their own process via reflection. Projects and people differ so much, it is hard to define a process to support all of them. A process will support everybody much better if it can be adjusted to fit the individual needs of team members.

Sometimes, people seem to believe that when developing a project with a large team, rules have to be put in place and strictly enforced. Conversely, with a small team, the typical strategy is to lead with simple common sense. /

Processes Masquerading As Agile

Agile processes are trendy. That is why everybody wants to label all their products and services as "agile." Furthermore, the Manifesto is written in a way in which it is very difficult to disagree. Even hardcore linear-process fans will, for example, agree that people are the most important subject in project development. Therefore, glancing at the Manifesto will not really help to characterize an agile process. On top of that, there are no formal, explicit, and hard criteria that define an agile process. This makes it easy to sell every process as an agile one. Some of the agile processes are defined in every detail, but since they serve as a starting line and can (and should) be adapted according to the team's needs, they can change over time. Consequently, they may change during the course of the development cycle, so that they no longer reflect their original definition.

Extreme Programming is an agile process that has a very detailed definition. Because of this, one can hardly follow another process and claim that it is Extreme Programming. But Extreme Programming can also be adapted. This dilemma was the basis for an anecdote Alistair Cockburn once told about people who followed *almost* Extreme Programming:

**Almost Extreme Programming
by Alistair Cockburn**[10]

Extreme Programming (à la Chrysler Comprehensive Compensation project) requires four things:[11]

- You do pair programming.
- You deliver an increment every three weeks.
- You have a user on the team full-time.
- You have regression unit tests that pass 100 percent of the time.

As a reward for doing those,

- You do not put comments in the code.
- You do not write any requirements or design documentation.

---

[10]This anecdote can be found at http://c2.com/cgi/wiki?AlmostExtremePro gramming.

[11]Chrysler Comprehensive Compensation was the first Extreme Programming project world-wide. See http://c2.com/cgi/wiki?ChryslerComprehen siveCompensation.

> Now, on this project, we're pretty close . . .
>
> - Well, actually, a couple of our guys sit in the basement, a couple on the 5th floor, and a couple two hours' drive from here, so we do not do pair programming.
> - Actually, we deliver our increments every four to six months.
> - We do not have users anywhere in sight, and we do not have any unit tests.
>
> But at least *we do not have any design documentation, and we do not comment on our code much!* So, in a sense, we're *almost* doing Extreme Programming!

With agile processes other than Extreme Programming, things can get even worse. First of all, they are not well known, so not a lot of people have the skills necessary to tell if the process really follows the specified agile process. Another reason is that it is not easy to get a detailed, consistent description of most other agile processes, because some of their descriptions are spread over a couple of articles and Websites. In contrast, there are numerous books available on the subject of Extreme Programming. Therefore, if an organization wants to follow an agile process other than Extreme Programming, it is absolutely necessary to scrutinize the process (actually, I would recommend this for any process applied, agile or not).

As mentioned earlier, there are not a lot of criteria available on which to judge a process, especially if a nameless agile process is put into action. By "nameless," I mean one that is not an official representative of agile processes. The only basis for identifying agile processes is the set of four main characteristics described by the Agile Manifesto. Use the following questions as a guideline:

- Do the project members contribute to shaping the process? Furthermore, are the members able to adapt the process so it gives them optimal support? Is changing the process easy, or does it require overcoming a lot of obstacles?
- Do all project members know the purpose of each of the artifacts (documents, diagrams, prototypes, and the like)?

For example, what is the purpose of each document? Who needs it? What for? Who develops it, and when? How does the document contribute to reaching the goal of always having a running system available?

- Do the members of the project know their customer (or group of customers)? Is there a customer delegate available to help clarify the requirements? If the delegate is a surrogate, does he or she have relevant experience? Is there any risk that he or she may make false assumptions about the requirements of the customer?

- What happens when requirements change? Do people try to eliminate them through discussion? Does every change require a massive change in the underlying architecture? Does the contract allow the team to deal flexibly with changed requirements and the scope of the project?

People Shape the Process

Switching to an agile process always implies a big change. In order for team members to accept the change, their hopes and fears must be respected. Therefore, you have to carefully watch the members of the project when introducing any kind of change. Otherwise, the change may cause you to lose more than you gain. Thus, the process you are using must constantly adapt to the needs of the people using it. The best way to figure out what their needs are is by communicating with them extensively and directly, and by respecting the concerns they voice.

Culture of Change

An article published recently in the German magazine *DAV Panorama,* about human (mis)behavior, compared the behavior of mackerels with that of humans.[12]

The results were astonishing:

- Mackerels and human beings normally show a similar reaction if they are in a large group.

---

[12]Peer van der Helm and Dieter Stopper, "Von Makrelen und Menschen" ("About Mackerels and Human Beings"), *DAV Panorama*, No. 1, Issue 54 (2002), pp. 51–52.

- If mackerels or humans are starving, they react irrationally. For example, if a mackerel is hungry, it is much easier to catch with a fishing rod; similarly, especially poor people may be more likely to gamble in lotteries.
- Both mackerels and humans are creatures of habit. Mackerels have lots of habits and *always* follow them. People also have lots of habits and have great *difficulty* in not always following them.

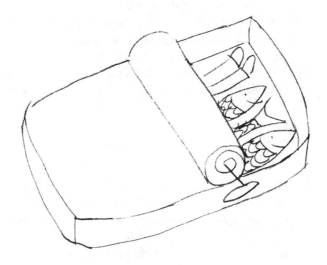

Human beings and mackerels ...

The crucial difference between mackerels and humans is that we humans have a cerebrum, which allows us to make decisions. The major decision we can make is to break our habits—to try a new path or to give something up in order to make room for something else.

Culture often hinders our willingness to change habits. Culture is a way of thinking, developed over time and taught to new members of a community as *the* way of thinking. So, culture influences the way we behave. Moreover, culture helps us deal with reality and reduces uncertainty at the same time, giving us stability and confidence. Furthermore, culture is the identity of a community. It makes our community more understandable, and this is why it is so difficult to give up or change our culture.

If we examine our corporate culture in more detail, we will find the following:

- **Obvious signs:** Tools, scripts, magazines, and war stories. Many people who are counted as heroes are known for taking risks but seldom known for having successfully finished a single project. In their war stories, you will rarely find an instance of misbehavior or wrong decisions. On the other hand, we learn a lot from our failures, so a person who does not admit failure may fail to learn.

- **Values:** Values are communicated via books and training courses. But how many people respect the wisdom contained therein? For example, the first edition of Tom DeMarco and Timothy Lister's book *Peopleware* was written in 1987, but how much have we learned?[13] We still make the same mistakes when working together on teams.

- **Fundamental assumptions:** What everybody is convinced is necessary and desirable. The following cultural assumptions influence our expectations of projects.

  - **Truth and reality:** Often, we claim something but act in a way that completely contradicts this claim. For example, we know that tests are our safety nets, but too often, people still do not develop them. Or, even if they do, tests are the first thing to be canceled when the team finds itself running out of time.

  - **Human behavior:** Often, we follow other people, mainly so-called authorities. In groups, the accepted authority is more often known for his or her self-assertion, not his or her professional qualifications. Or, sometimes we follow the local habits without consideration. For example, in many companies, working overtime is a status symbol. If you do not work overtime, you are seen as less important and as not having anything serious to do. Consequently, people work overtime even if it is unnecessary. (This happens less often in large companies; the employees would get in trouble with the staff association—in Europe, anyway.)

---

[13]Tom DeMarco and Timothy Lister, *Peopleware: Productive Projects and Teams* (New York: Dorset House Publishing, 1st ed. 1987, 2nd ed. 1999).

Another strange example is the finish-effect: At the end of the day or at the end of a project, as the project reaches its final stages, people tend to accept much riskier designs if they involve a lighter workload. Conversely, something with less risk but a greater workload will be ignored, even though it would probably be much more understandable and easier to maintain.

Human Frailty is Admonished

- **Human relations:** Everybody wants to be regarded as strong, capable, and clever. To admit that we need help from our peers or that our own design needs further refinement is not easy for most people.

- **Heroism:** Some people, so-called authorities, try to be especially clever. They invent designs that can only be understood by themselves and the computer. They do this because they assume that writing code that is too convoluted for their peers to understand is a way of showing off how clever they are. The problem here is that their peers often admire the cleverness instead of making the obvious point that the design should be understandable not only to the computer, but also to anyone who might have to read it. I remember a T-shirt fashionable among C programmers that had the following printed on it, in a huge font:

  **(++p[-1]) *= x++++++y;
  /* You are not supposed to understand this */

  I have to admit I'm not sure I remember the coding statement right, but I remember the phrase—a sure sign that I was not supposed to understand this (which I did not).

Everybody is unconsciously influenced by his or her own thoughts and actions, especially when confronted with a difficult situation. Therefore, ask yourself occasionally if you are acting like a human being or a mackerel.

27

Adaptation

There is no process that is a perfect fit for any organization, project, or team. Agile processes are no exception. This means that you have to adapt each process in order for your project to be successful. Or, as Martin Fowler put it,

> We must be completely inflexible on where we want to go, but completely flexible on how we get there.[14]

This means that it is not enough to embrace the changes to your customer's requirements. You must also evolve and make the necessary modifications to the process, and welcome them. The ability to do this comes from retrospectives. However, you have to allow time for yourself, your team, and your company to embrace the change. Do not overreact if something is not working immediately, because introducing a new process always incurs a cost in time, a change, and even more important, the usual initial reaction to every change—rejection.

Installing an agile process is a major change on its own. You can use an existing agile process as a starting line, and modify it according to your needs. But you have to carefully decide if you need to change the starting line because of the resistance you encountered toward installing an agile process or because the process in its current form really does not suit the people's needs. Of course, it is important to counter this resistance to change, and the most effective way to do that is to improve the way in which the change is introduced.

An agile process can be extremely helpful in spotting the problems buried in the teams. As Dierk König concluded,

> Extreme Programming often works as a trouble detector.[15]

---

[14]Martin Fowler, "Is Analysis Dead?" (International Conference on eXtreme Programming and Agile Processes in Software-Engineering 2001, Sardinia, Italy, 2001).

[15]See http://c2.com/cgi/wiki?ExtremeProgrammingAsTroubleDetector.

For example, if team members refuse to work in pairs, this could be a sign that they have communication problems and do not respect each other.

Never introduce everything at once, because this will more than likely overwhelm all those involved. Introduce the process one step at a time and always address the most pressing problem first. If, for example, the rate of bugs is unbearably high, start by unit testing, followed by refactoring (which I discuss in more detail later in this chapter). Hopefully, you already have coding standards in place, but maybe they are too complex or formalized and act as guardians for the developers instead of giving the support necessary to create a good design. If this is the case, invite the developers to simplify the coding standards first. They will let you know what they really need. This is the precondition for the acceptance of the coding standards. Pair-programming often helps in implementing the coding standards and reducing the error rate.

Introducing new processes is a slow process—introduce them one technique at a time. Only once the first technique becomes a habit should you introduce the next one. You have to be patient, even if you are sure that the specific change would really help the whole team. Bear in mind that the team might not be ready for the change. Instead of gratefully accepting the change, team members might reject it and any subsequent ideas you may have that would benefit the team. The best strategy for introducing a change is to discuss it with your team members and let them have a say in how the change will be implemented, so that during this communication, the change evolves into one that is acceptable to all concerned. Of course, in doing so, you can guide them toward the idea you have in mind. But if they do not see the problem, they will not accept the solution.

All these techniques require a lot of discipline, as with the learning of any other technique. Take tennis, for example. The sport itself does not require discipline; flexibility and creativity are required to win the game. But it takes discipline to learn the basic techniques of the sport, and to train yourself in them until they become instinct. Once you have mastered this, it is no longer a case of discipline, but of using the learned techniques flexibly and creatively. Similarly, creative and innovative teams are not best supported by rigorous methods, because they do not provide any freedom for creativity, flexibility, or innovation.

Avoid the temptation to make changes to your process just because you *think* there might be a problem. Make changes only when necessary, but always keep an eye on those areas that are known as trouble spots in the company. Being on the lookout for problems before they arise gives you a better chance of catching them in time, rather than reacting—or overreacting—when it is too late.

Communication

It seems that almost no project fails due to a specific technology, tool, or the like. The main reason for project failure is almost always a problem with, or a lack of, communication. The term "communication" covers interactions between team members, between different teams, between teams and management, between teams and customers, and so on. Furthermore, it is a fact that no communication is as efficient as direct communication. The efficiency of direct or face-to-face communication is reinforced by the layout of your office. The efficiency of communication, and therefore of the project, is proportional to how close the project members sit to each other. Alistair Cockburn explains this effect in great detail in *Agile Software Development,* in which he details the effects an office layout has on communication costs within a project:

- the lost-opportunity cost of not asking questions
- the overall cost of detecting and transferring information
- the reduction in cost when people discover information in background sounds[16]

Sometimes, a communication structure, which has to be installed via direct communication, works for a while, even when using indirect channels. But often, the efficiency of the communication will begin to suffer. For example, the effort it takes to write an e-mail or make a phone call to get an answer to a tiny little question is often regarded as too much to be worth the trouble. Willingness to use these forms of indirect communication drops fast, much like

---

[16]Alistair Cockburn, *Agile Software Development* (Reading, Mass.: Addison-Wesley, 2002), p. 81.

the rate of response. Imagine if it takes a day to get an answer to your e-mail, or you find the phone busy each time you try to reach your colleague—chances are, at some point, you will simply give up. This typically leads everybody to make assumptions or to wait until the next opportunity for direct communication. However, by that time, the question is not only forgotten, it will already have been answered with an assumption.

Alistair Cockburn lists the different modalities of communication, in increasing order of effectiveness:

- paper
- audio tape
- two people on e-mail
- video tape
- two people on phone
- two people at a whiteboard[17]

The strange thing is that most projects still stick to the least effective communication channel—paper—instead of considering a different office layout.

Mistrust in Applicability

Agile software development often sounds so simple that a lot of people cannot believe that it could possibly work. The typical reaction to mistrust in an approach is to ask the team to deliver a set of defined artifacts or to use particular tools. In all honesty, we know that everybody can produce almost any artifact—other than code—or can use any kind of tool. However, the production of the artifact or the usage of the tool is not a sign that the system has reached a specific status. The only sign that leads to this conclusion is working software.

This section focuses on two kinds of techniques: First, we discuss techniques that are often used for overcoming mistrust in processes and teams. Then, we discuss techniques that are quite common in agile software development but often lead to mistrust in non-agile environments.

---

[17]Ibid. p. 95.

Documentation

There is a myth that some agile methodologies regard documentation as being evil. This may stem from the Agile Manifesto's preference for "working software over comprehensive documentation." This has sometimes been interpreted to mean that nobody who follows an agile methodology documents a thing. The truth is, documentation is considered very carefully in agile methodologies, especially when compared to a more document-centered methodology. Current documentation has to be thoroughly examined.

The documentation I find in most non-agile projects is write-only. Write-only documentation is easy to spot: It looks very accurate, stays on the shelf, and has no coffee stains on any page. This is a clear sign that nobody really trusts it. This is understandable. Documentation is not executable and thus not testable. Therefore, it is difficult to judge whether or not it really describes the things you are looking for.

But why do people produce so much documentation? A lot of people are afraid to have no documentation (or not enough), which again is a result of the expectations people have about documentation. So the key question arises, What do people hope documentation will offer? The answer is simple: knowledge transfer. And the concern is that this knowledge will otherwise be lost somewhere along the way. To be more precise, people expect documentation to provide the following:

- **Transfer of knowledge between the customer and the developer,** better known as requirements documentation.

  However, according to Jim Highsmith, requirements documentation is, on average, only 15-percent complete and 7-percent correct.[18] Obviously, requirements documentation does not usually meet expectations, but it is still developed. And despite the poor quality of the requirements documents, a functional piece of software is often the end product (well, sometimes, at least). How, you ask? Another

---

[18]James A. Highsmith III, "Agile Methodologies: Problems, Principles and Practices" (International Conference on eXtreme Programming and Agile Processes in Software-Engineering 2001, Sardinia, Italy, 2001).

kind of knowledge transfer exists between customers and developers, and it is not based on documentation.

- **Transfer of knowledge between newcomers and veterans,** better known as design and code documentation.

This path of knowledge transfer is focused more on development and maintenance, and less on customer acceptance. The biggest hope regarding this knowledge transfer is that the design and code documentation will be able to transfer the necessary knowledge even if the veterans are long gone. Unfortunately, if that is the situation, and there is a need for newcomers to understand the system, the documentation will not be much help. Like requirements documents, code and design documents are rarely complete, up-to-date, or easy to understand.

According to Fred Brooks, the solution to this problem is

> . . . to merge files, to incorporate the documentation in the source program. This is at once a powerful incentive toward proper maintenance, and an insurance that the documentation will always be handy to the program user. Such programs are called self-documenting.[19]

Aside from a few exceptions, veterans are usually not around to train newcomers, and the design and code documentation is often rather lousy. Despite this, however, it is not uncommon for newcomers to enter a project successfully. Therefore, there must be a way of transferring knowledge that actually works. We will look at this successful knowledge transfer later on.

But the question remains: Why do people still insist on these kinds of documentation, even though it is common knowledge that they are rarely of a high enough quality to be effective? The answer is fear: Everybody produces these documents under the assumption that all other projects have quality documentation (unlike them-

---

[19]Frederick P. Brooks, Jr., *The Mythical Man-Month: Essays on Software Engineering*, 20th anniv. ed. (Reading, Mass.: Addison-Wesley, 1995), p. 169.

selves). If this assumption did not exist, nobody would write these documents, but would instead develop another, more successful way of transferring knowledge. Of course, if you were actually to use a different knowledge transfer and it didn't work, you would shoulder the blame (unlike when traditional documentation doesn't work—that is the norm). However, if you switch to an agile process, you could also consider revising the style of knowledge transfer.

Agile development fosters all kinds of documentation that helps its users achieve their goal of producing *working software*. Or, as Alistair Cockburn put it in his discussion of development as a cooperative game,

> The purpose of the game is to deliver software. Any other activity is secondary. A model, as any communication, is sufficient, as soon as it permits the next person to move on with her work.[20]

Therefore, you will use all kinds of documentation in an agile process. However, most often, you will find that these documents are in support of communication. This is actually the reason that agile developers are able to transfer knowledge despite the poor quality of traditional documentation. For example, newcomers often ignore the official documents but instead talk to their peers and look at the piece of documentation that is always up-to-date—the code.

As Pete McBreen observed in *Software Craftsmanship,* instead of promoting cross-training among developers,

> . . . software engineering promotes the myth that what is needed instead is good documentation. Unfortunately, although documentation is very good for recording decisions and agreements, it is a very ineffective way of preserving and communicating detailed knowledge of how a software application actually works.[21]

---

[20]Cockburn, op. cit., p. 30.

[21]Pete McBreen, *Software Craftsmanship: The New Imperative* (Reading, Mass.: Addison-Wesley, 2002), p. 124.

So you need to find the courage to eliminate the traditional documents, which are developed for self-preservation only and do not assist you in the achievement of your ultimate goal. As a substitute—and here comes the hard part—you have to foster different kinds of communication in order to ensure the knowledge transfer. In agile processes, you will hardly find any "dead" documents, but you will find a lot of vivid documentation. It might not look as pretty as traditional documents, but the probability that it is up-to-date is almost infinitely greater.

Design

People sometimes fear that a system will not be designed if the team follows an agile process. This fear is misplaced—the system will of course be designed. However, with agile projects, the design is often expressed differently than people expect.

Generally, each design has different views. These different views are expressed with different notations. For example, the most common views are those expressed in source code and Unified Modeling Language (UML). Because these are just different views of the same thing, design or modeling are rarely explicitly mentioned in this book. Therefore, whenever something is implemented, there is an implication that it has been designed, which in turn means it was modeled in some way and coded. So, code often gets created after the design has been modeled, for example, in UML. The design might be modeled on different levels and expressed with different notations, but this has no impact on the big picture or on the progress and success of the project. The main goal stays the same: to produce working software, not documents.

UML documents often have the same problems as all other documents: They are seldom complete and rarely up-to-date. But you can decide for yourself if this is really a problem: The UML document did fulfill its purpose—it helped team members to come up with a proper design. If, let's say, the design changes, and this change is only reflected in the source code, not in the UML document, this should not be a problem since the document has already served its purpose and no longer contributes anything toward reaching our goal. As Scott Ambler puts it,

> Once a model has fulfilled its goals you should stop work-
> ing on it—you are finished![22]

Later on, he adds,

> You should update an artifact such as a model or document
> only when you absolutely need to, when not having the model
> updated is more painful than the effort of updating it.[23]

But if for some reason an up-to-date UML document is necessary,

- Do not insist on updating all the UML documents along the
  way. It will be difficult to motivate people to do this, as it
  no longer has any immediate purpose and it does not help
  to produce working software.
- Look for a tool or write a script that will always produce a
  current UML document from the existing code. This will
  give you the graphical view of the actual design.

Testing

A common and reasonable fear is that testing will slow development down. While this is definitely true at the very start of a project, having tests available will accelerate the development later on,
when the system requires some changes.

Agile methodologies emphasize early testing. Tests are generally used as a safety net for functionality and stability. They serve
their main purpose during development. If the tests are developed
after development, as is quite common practice in the industry,
they are not much use. This is why a lot of people do not like to
test—they don't see the point. Having tests available early on,
however, simplifies, or rather enables, changes to the system under
development. You always have a guarantee that whatever you
changed did not affect the system negatively.

Generally, tests are not of much use if they are not run after
every change. Furthermore, they are useless if failure is accepted.
Living with failed tests (even just one) is the same as living without

---

[22]Scott Ambler, *Agile Modeling: Effective Practices for Extreme Programming & the
Unified Process* (New York: John Wiley & Sons, 2002), p. 32.
[23]Ibid. p. 67.

any tests, because only one small tear is enough to let everything slip through the safety net.

Tests …

ACCEPTANCE OR FUNCTIONAL TEST

Better known as black-box tests, acceptance tests ensure the functionality of the system.[24] Typically, they are based on the requirements, which means that they can often be developed in parallel to the code. It is a good idea for the customer to create the acceptance tests, to at least be a part of the acceptance test team. Acceptance tests are also very important after integration, because they ensure that the system still works as it should and that the different integrated subsystems do not have any unwanted effects on each other.

---

[24]Acceptance tests are sometimes also known as system tests. However, the official meaning of "system test" is "integration test."

Their main purpose, however, is to ensure that the requirements are met. This way, they can serve as a very precise specification for the requirements. This is why it is so beneficial to have the customer develop them or to assist in their development.

UNIT TEST

Unit tests are typically created by the developers. This is the main safety net for refactoring and for introducing new features. Some agile methodologies (Extreme Programming being the main one) prefer to develop the unit tests before the code. This helps the developers understand the interface, the expected functionality, and the limitations of the code, and therefore helps them to develop the code. Developing the tests first, before the code, is generally regarded as more of a design technique than a development one. Thus, unit tests help the developer design the code better, which makes the code easier to expand on, later in the project. This is very important in relation to refactoring, as detailed in the next section.

When do you develop a test?

- For each unit: A typical unit is a class.
- With the occurrence of a bug: First, develop the test that produces the bug, then eliminate the bug. The test makes sure the bug is eliminated and that, in the future, it will not reoccur.
- When something is difficult to understand: If the interface is not clear, the implementation seems to be difficult, or there are unusual arguments and side conditions required, a unit test helps reduce the complexity.

But do not insist on testing for trivialities; otherwise, the developers are likely to stop writing tests altogether. On the other hand, colleagues of mine insist on writing tests even for trivial methods, like the ones for setting and retrieving an attribute of an object. The main reason is to get rid of unnecessary discussions about which methods are trivial and which are not.

Besides acting as a safety net, unit tests are the best documentation of the source code, and they are always up-to-date (provided the tests do not fail).

AUTOMATED TESTS

No matter what kinds of tests we are talking about, they must be automated. Otherwise, the risk is high that

- people will not test, because it has too great an effort cost
- people will not test properly and will not be able to tell whether the system still does today what it did yesterday

Different kinds of support is available for automating tests: scripts, test frameworks, or test tools. You can find for almost any programming language tools that are freely available for both unit and acceptance tests.[25]

Refactoring

Refactoring is best described by quoting Martin Fowler from his book *Refactoring: Improving the Design of Existing Code:*

> Refactoring is the process of changing a software system in such a way that it does not alter the external behavior of the code yet improves its internal structure. . . . In essence when you refactor you are improving the design of the code after it has been written.[26]

This means that refactoring can start as soon as any code has been written. If the code is to be understood not only by the computer but also by humans, there is no way around refactoring. However, some people have expressed their fear that refactoring increases the development and testing effort, and therefore increases the total cost and length of the project.

---

[25]For general test tools, see http://c2.com/cgi/wiki?TestingFramework; for unit tests, see http://www.junit.org/; for acceptance tests, see http://fit.c2.com/.

[26]Martin Fowler, *Refactoring: Improving the Design of Existing Code* (Reading, Mass.: Addison-Wesley, 1999), p. xvi.

Typically, refactoring is an ongoing task done by everybody on the team. But people have to be sure that they are either refactoring or implementing a new feature. Doing both at once makes it impossible for there to be a guarantee that the refactoring will only improve the internal structure of the system, and will not unintentionally change its external behavior. The risk is too high that afterward, the system will not work the way it did before.

Why is refactoring so important?

- It helps prevent the ruin of software.
- It is essential for any evolutionary development process. If development is done incrementally, there must be a defined way to change the existing system.
- Agile development fosters learning during development. Refactoring allows us to apply what we learn, as we learn it, to the existing system.
- Refactoring helps us find bugs.

Refactoring is much easier if done with a tool. Furthermore, it is essential to have a safety net of unit tests available, to ensure that after the refactoring, the system still does what it ought to and that nothing breaks.

When do you refactor—if not continuously?

- when some constructions in the code point at problems (the code smells—see below)
- when introducing new functionality is difficult
- when the code review discovers some problems
- when elimination of bugs makes refactoring obviously necessary

In general, a refactoring is always required as soon as the existing code *smells*. Experience helps to detect these smells, but also simple indications (long functions or procedures, complex nestings, or just difficulty understanding the code). Code reviews help to uncover those indications. If adding new functionality is difficult, you have found another source for refactoring. Instead of adding this functionality immediately, you should prepare the code by making it simpler. Other hints are bugs that keep occurring in the same areas of the system. This is a sure sign that these areas desperately need a refactoring.

Some people are afraid to implement a refactoring effort in certain situations, such as when you have elements in your system that are difficult to change, like a database schema. You can still refactor these parts, but only if you encapsulate them, as required by layered architectures. Another difficult change that people are reluctant to perform is a refactoring required in an interface. You can easily undertake this refactoring if the code that uses the interface is accessible. Otherwise, you do have the problem of backward compatibility. So, if this code is not accessible, keep the old interface, but call it deficient so everybody using the interface is aware that something has changed.

Summary

The Agile Manifesto formulates a value system for software development. Even though it provides a fundamental definition of lightweight, agile methods, it is not very explicit and leaves room for interpretation. This freedom leaves open the risk that heavyweight processes will be peddled as agile processes. Yet the use of an agile process exhibits a clear change in the culture and the ability to adapt as necessary.

Switching to agile development may arouse some fears, which in turn could foster mistrust in the success of the approach. Although some artifacts and tools promise putative security for controlling and steering a project, this security is just that—putative. It is much more important to establish an environment of trust, which will allow open and honest communication even if the project is in bad shape. Trust can only be built by transparency, consistency, and integrity.

In order to ensure the provision of a system with the highest possible business value, developers must work very closely with their customers during project development. This involvement not only helps the developers to better understand the requirements, it also helps the customer determine what kind of system would best meet the business's needs.

3

AGILITY AND LARGE TEAMS

Trust is the sister of responsibility.
    —Asian proverb

The reasons for implementing a system with a large team are varied. The most common one is that the scope of the project is too large for a small team to handle. However, some large projects would be better off if implemented by a small team. Even if the scope is large, a small team may be faster or more effective, mainly because communication is not as likely to prove a problem as it is in a large team.

Sometimes, the use of a large team is politically motivated. The size of a team may signify the importance of the project and of the project management itself. Author and consultant Tom DeMarco discussed this problem during OOPSLA 2001.[1] He indicated that surprisingly often, the manager of a failed but large project will be valued higher than the manager of a successful but small project.

Furthermore, the project may be shaped and sized to suit a team that is already established. For instance, I witnessed a situation in an organization where a lot of people just sat around, waiting for the project to start. Nobody questioned if this mass of people was really required for the project. Instead, everybody tried to shape the project in a way that kept all these people busy. Granted,

---

[1]OOPSLA is an ACM SIGPLAN conference: Object-Oriented Programming, Systems, Languages, and Applications.

for some companies (in some countries), it might be easier to shape the project according to the team's size than to get rid of the employees—mainly because of legal issues—but this is not usually the case.

It is always worth questioning the reasons for working with a large team, but this is neither the topic of the book in general nor of this chapter in particular. Instead, the assumption is that the project will be run by a large team and you want to use an agile process. When changing to agile development with a *large* team, you have to deal with several issues involving people, teams, interactions, and communication structures.

This chapter focuses on those aspects of agile processes that work differently in large teams than in smaller teams. First, we look at the people aspect. We discuss how taking up responsibility can work in a large team and what kind of consequences respect, acceptance, and trust have for successful collaboration. Next, we consider how a large team can be divided into subteams and what kind of team roles have to be occupied. In the section on interaction and communication structures, we focus on encouraging communication in large teams. Then, in the section on trouble-shooting, I present typical team problems and their possible solutions. Finally, we look at the difficulties that can occur when developing with dispersed teams.

People

Size matters. The size of a team provides a special risk—a team that is too large can hinder a project. One reason is that the quality of the decision-making typically suffers. For example, the larger the team, the more often you will find that decisions are unclear or postponed. The main reason for this is that within large teams, you will often find a tendency among people to shun responsibility. Because there are so many people on the team, there is a collective mentality that "someone else will decide."

Unclear or postponed decisions confuse the team and make it difficult for team members to decide which direction to take. This leads either to project paralysis, because nobody has the courage to move on without being told, or to a lot of individual decisions as one thinks best. Often, those individual decisions contradict each other, which in turn leads to a form of project stagnation, based on contradictory development. Both symptoms are very frustrating for the whole team. I once consulted on a restart of a failed project. I interviewed team members about what trap they believed would most likely ensnare the restart. Interestingly enough, most people named a lack of clear decisions as the highest risk.

Therefore, although it might seem unusual, it is preferable to make a clear but eventually wrong decision and to correct it later. Making a wrong decision enables you to learn; postponing a decision does not. If you postpone a decision, you do not know until it has been made whether it is the right or the wrong one. However, if you make the wrong decision, you will learn from the consequences and will have the possibility of correcting your mistake, based on your new experience.

Making decisions is one side of the coin; the other is making sure that they are not only communicated to everybody involved but are also carried out. A decision that is made but not carried out is essentially the same as a postponed decision.

Although this all sounds very obvious, it is common to find the same problems popping up over and over again, which is a sure sign that those decisions either have never been clearly made or have not been realized.

As I mentioned earlier, the main reason for the poor quality of decisions on projects with large teams is probably based on an aversion to taking responsibility. You will find that the more people there are, the harder it is to tell who took responsibility for which task. Often, this results in an *undefined task zone*, which is defined by

- **Multiplicated task responsibility:** A lot of people are responsible for the same task. The problem is that they do not know about one another. Therefore, if you are lucky, this task will be carried out repeatedly. If you are unfortunate, they will do the task in ways that contradict each other.
- **Null task responsibility:** Nobody takes responsibility for the task. Everybody assumes that it is someone else's job. This can result in everybody blaming everybody else for not taking the responsibility.

To make things worse, you can be assured that with each additional team member, the risk will rise and more of such problems will arise.

Responsibility

Due to the departmental organization, people in large companies are not usually used to having complete responsibility for any particular task. This is because there is almost always somebody higher up the hierarchy who has *ultimate* responsibility. This is especially true for developers. They often see themselves as only doing what somebody else tells them. When somebody "accidentally" gives them the responsibility for a specific task, they feel uncertain. They are not used to having responsibility, and they do not know what it implies.

On the other hand, agile processes require everybody to be responsible for his or her task, and for the effects that task might have on the whole project. In addition to individual tasks, there is also the shared responsibility for the ultimate performance of the whole system, the project, and even the process of development. Thus, each team member is responsible in some way for every task, even those assigned to other team members.

For example, Extreme Programming has a practice called *collective ownership*, which refers to a shared responsibility for all kinds of things: the code, the integration, the process, and so on. Best known among these shared responsibilities is probably collective code ownership, which enables and obliges everybody on the team to improve every piece of code, no matter whether he or she is the original author of the code or not.

With collective ownership, every team member bears the same responsibility for all aspects of the project. However, allowing everybody to steer the project at the same time is a challenge and, some fear, a big burden. For instance, every developer would want to have a hand in shaping his or her development environment. At the same time, this increased responsibility is likely to increase the developers' fear of making the wrong decisions.

When people first sign up for a task but aren't used to the responsibility it entails, you have to lead them gently into this new territory. For example, ask the developers which task they want to be responsible for, and then assist them in estimating the task. Not only should you make yourself available to answer any questions they may have, it is very important that you also ask them regularly if they are doing okay, or if they need any help, because they might be afraid to bring up such issues themselves.

For example, I remember one project I was working on, where people had problems taking responsibility. I visited all the team members regularly and asked them how they were getting along with their tasks. It did not take long before some of them started complaining that they were not able to get their work done, for various reasons. The most common reply was that they were waiting for something from another team: either the other team had not yet provided some interfaces, or the interface it had provided turned out to be different than expected.

The obvious problem was that these people did not have the right mindset for problem-solving. Instead, they complained that their peers were responsible for the problems. The real, hidden problem was that they were not taking enough responsibility. If they had, they would not have complained, but rather would have started solving their problems. In other words, they might have started talking to this other team, found out why the interfaces were not ready, and addressed the situation.

The typical reaction of people not used to responsibility is to get annoyed at the situation without taking any action to change it. Of course, it could be worse. If, for instance, they could neither complain nor take up the responsibility, you would never learn about their problems.

Therefore, you have to be proactive in asking developers about the status of their assigned task. Only then will you have an idea of any problems they may have. I'm not talking about status reports—I'm talking about walking up to the people and talking face-to-face about their current situation. You should encourage them to look at the big picture and regard their assigned task as part of the whole. Explain that even tasks that may only be partly related to their assigned task (if at all) are important for the completion of the project.

If people are spoon-fed responsibility, they will not learn to make an effort to take it up themselves. Or, as an article in *Fast Company* put it,

> Telling people what to do doesn't guarantee that they will
> learn enough to think for themselves in the future. Instead,
> it may mean that they'll depend on you or their superiors
> even more and that they will stop taking chances, stop
> innovating, stop learning.[2]

Telling people what to do is not enough. They have to commit themselves to their task. The focal point of this philosophy is that the value of team productivity is much more important than the individual effort. Therefore, every now and then, you have to point out that only the team's success is the individual's success. An individual's success without the success of the team is of no value. Among other things, this means that a well-functioning team does not rely on its official manager—it takes up the responsibility itself, whenever the situation requires it. For this approach to become a reality, the organization has to change from management by command and control to management by responsibility, trust, and teamwork.

Trust is the foundation on which such a management strategy is built. When someone takes on a responsibility, you trust that he or she is capable of handling that responsibility. However, at the start of an organization's first agile project, this culture of trust and responsibility will not be in place yet. Most team members will not be able to take up responsibility, because they are not used to it. However, I suggest that you demonstrate to them how you take up responsibility, and that you encourage them to take responsibility even if they do not feel ready. This shows your team members that you trust them, even though at this early stage in agile development they might not be able to justify your trust. When you refrain from giving them any responsibility, you prevent them from ever getting the chance to learn how to take up responsibility. That simply reinforces their own mistrust in their capabilities. Just as Ulrich Sollmann and Roderich Heinze say, you should give people the chance to learn how to deal with responsibility:

---

[2]Chuck Salter, "Attention Class!!! 16 Ways to Be a Smarter Teacher," *Fast Company*, Issue 53 (December 2001), p. 114.

The more often you are in an uncertain situation, the better you can handle this kind of situation, or rather the longer it will take till you will again feel uncertain.[3]

If you want to train your team members to take up responsibility, you have to be aware that this is an investment in their future. This "training" is two-sided: You may also have to train leaders to delegate responsibility and to trust their team members. As with every other learning process, it will be some time before you see results, but it is worth the effort.

Respect and Acceptance

A development team is not usually organized like a team, in the strictest sense of the word—assembled by peers with equal rights—it's hierarchical. The typical hierarchy in a development team, found mainly in traditionally led projects, follows Taylor's theory about centralizing a team's knowledge.[4] Individual team members take up specific roles and corresponding tasks. Analysts, designers, developers, and testers often work independently in a linear process.

As a consequence of this separation of tasks and roles, a hierarchy is created. Although perhaps not officially sanctioned, the hierarchy is formed by the different roles in the team, some of which have greater prestige, importance, or acceptance level than others. Often, the acceptance level is defined by the linear development. This means that analysts have the highest acceptance level, while coders, testers, and, even worse, maintainers are at the very end of the acceptance-level chain, doing all the dirty work. This sequence of acceptance levels is just one example, but an oft-encountered one.

The major problem is that nobody wants to be at the low end of this acceptance-level chain. Therefore (as in the example above),

---

[3]Ulrich Sollmann and Roderich Heinze, *Visionsmanagement: Erfolg als vorausgedachtes Ergebnis* (*Vision Management: Success as the Predefined Result*) (Zürich: Orell Füssli, 1994), p. 32.

[4]Taylorism is characterized by the division of labor, repetitive operations, extreme labor discipline, and the supervision of work.

everybody tries to climb up the ladder from maintainer to designer or, even better, analyst. From another perspective, you will find the largest percentage of novices in maintenance or implementation. Consequently, there are often too few experienced coders on a team.

In contrast, most agile processes require teams to have shared knowledge and shared skills. This means knowledge cannot serve to form a hierarchy. Therefore, the first step in forming an agile team is to get rid of the Tayloristic split. Assemble teams that cover all the knowledge, where each member of the team is aware of the big picture and takes responsibility to contribute to the whole team's success. The individual role of each member is not so obvious, then, in terms of individual knowledge, but is recast in terms of contribution to the team's success. So, acceptance is then based on performance and not on roles.

One of the main differences between small and large agile teams is that in the former, every individual is typically requested to be a generalist. On the other hand, as I discuss later in this chapter, in a large agile team, a whole *subteam* and not necessarily every individual team member should cover this general knowledge.

This implies that agile teams require more generalists than specialists. At the least, everybody should be able and willing to understand the big picture and not become solely interested in digging into some specific details while ignoring the interests of the whole project.

So, as programmer and software expert Don Wells said, you will find that in an agile project,

Everyone is of equal value to the project.[5]

But this is only true if every team member bears responsibility for the whole project. Of course, each team member will have individual capabilities and abilities, but now he or she will contribute equally to the team and to the project.

---

[5]Don Wells, "Transitioning to XP or Fanciful Opinions of Don Wells," (International Conference on eXtreme Programming and Agile Processes in Software-Engineering 2001, Sardinia, Italy, 2001).

Trust

It is natural for people to be skeptical of a change like switching to an agile process. The team members themselves, along with a lot of people only partially involved in the project, might not have trust in the success of this new process. The possibility that the team can change the process over time is often even more frightening than following a defined but indigestible recipe.

The best argument against this mistrust is working software. Therefore, try to complete the first, low-functional version of the software as early as possible. Another strategy for building trust is transparency. Make everything transparent for everybody involved in the project.

Different practices help to make things more transparent:

- **Shared ownership:** Ask everybody on the team to take responsibility for all kinds of things (for instance, the code or the process). This shows your trust in them.
- **Shared knowledge:** This practice is often based on shared ownership. The knowledge about the information—for example, the system—is transferred from one team member to another. This makes the system more transparent and understandable for everybody, and helps in turn to build confidence in the system.
- **Shared skills:** The team has people with a variety of backgrounds and skills. This knowledge is accessible not only for the individuals, but for the whole team. Using non-agile processes, the individual guards expert knowledge from the whole team. Making knowledge transparent makes the team more trustworthy. Furthermore, it allows every team member to add new skills to their repertoire.

It is important that this transparency is always open and honest. Do not hide any negative information. Knowing about the bad things makes it easier to deal with them. Moreover, everybody should be invited to comment on the information and to help improve the situation. Thus, transparency includes representatives from control, audit, and, most importantly, the customer.

Occasionally, when coaching a project, I find that project members assume that transparency stops right before the customer. For example, I sometimes have to lead long discussions in order to open the project's wiki Web for the customer, because the customer will then have full access to the project.[6] Often, when asked for more transparency, project managers tell me they're afraid the customer will find out about the problems inside the project. This is exactly the point! The customer should always be aware of the problems, because the customer is paying for the project. These arguments are typical when discussing the impact of having the customer on-site. As soon as the customer becomes something of an unofficial project member, the fear disappears from both sides: from the team's side, because team members realize that the customer is a real person, and from the customer's side, because he or she understands the difficulties the project members are facing.

This reminds me of how I was before I started scuba diving: I liked swimming in the open sea, but I was always a bit afraid of the creatures underneath me, and I was pretty sure that sooner or later one of them would bite me. As soon as I started scuba diving, I did not even fear sharks or other predators. Being close to these creatures gave me the feeling of actually being a part of the living sea.

Team Building

A large team is hardly manageable as a whole. Thus, in order to establish a flexible team, the team is usually divided into subteams of no more than ten members.

The typical structure used by large teams (and in large companies) is still based on Taylor's theory of building teams according to their knowledge, as I mentioned earlier. Therefore, you will often find an analysis team, a design team, a test team, and so on. The developers are typically further subgrouped into smaller subteams, each responsible for a specific function like presentation, database, network services, and the like. This Tayloristic split is also known as *horizontal* team division. Taylorism works quite well for jobs that are repeatable. It doesn't work as well if a lot of cre-

---

[6]Originally developed by Ward Cunningham, a wiki Web is a Web-based collaboration platform that allows interactive communication and vivid documentation by editable HTML pages. See Bo Leuf and Ward Cunningham, *The Wiki Way: Collaboration and Sharing on the Internet* (Reading, Mass.: Addison-Wesley, 2001).

ative and holistic thinking is required. You can furthermore consider defining *vertical* teams, which are focused around business functionality. These teams are also known as domain or feature teams, as Peter Coad terms them in the Feature Driven Development process. On the other hand, if you are dividing the team vertically, you might find that not every team has all the necessary skills, or even worse, that every team might start to address the same problems.

Therefore, do not make this an *either-or* decision, but an *as-well-as* one. For example, if you start with a small team and build slowly, you will come to the conclusion that on future projects, your starting team should be staffed with people who have good domain knowledge and a major technical background. This starting team most often defines the first architecture and verifies that the system can actually be built. Furthermore, it can serve as a model for the formation of the other teams. The horizontal and more technically focused teams should then support these new (vertical) subteams.

Building Teams and Subteams

As mentioned earlier, dividing the whole team into several subteams should not be a decision between vertical *or* horizontal divisions. Instead, it should be an *as-well-as* decision, to provide a better mix of knowledge in the teams.

Either virtual or real technical service teams could be installed to further support those vertical, domain teams.[7] For example, on one of my projects, we defined domain teams focusing on a specific domain area in banking, with one team focusing on accounting and another one on customer management. Each team had the knowledge needed to implement the features belonging to its domain, including the graphical user interface, the connection to the host, the business logic, and all the other required technology. If, for instance, the accounting team required some functionality from the customer management team in order to implement a feature, the

---

[7]In some ways, a virtual team is not recognizable as a team. The team members may not be co-located, communicating only by electronic media, or the team members may in fact belong to different teams and just get together every now and then for work on a specific task.

accounting team would just bilaterally discuss the requirements with the customer management team. The customer management team then in turn would provide the required service within the development cycle.

Subteams …

We established in this case real (not virtual) technical service teams that were responsible for supporting the domain teams by providing some base functionality. For example, we assembled an architecture team responsible for the business logic, and a presentation team for all graphical user interface aspects. Those technical service teams were requested to visit all the domain teams regularly. On request, members of a technical service team supported domain teams as regular team members for a specific amount of time.

Technical service teams should always regard themselves as pure service providers for the domain teams. For instance, the technical service team responsible for building and supporting the architecture should always shape the architecture according to the requests of the domain teams, not vice versa, since the domain teams have to use whatever the architecture team creates, as is often the case.

Depending on the actual size of your team, you will establish either virtual technical service teams or real technical service teams. The members of the virtual teams are usually regular members of domain teams. In contrast, members of real teams usually lack a close connection to the domain teams. For this reason, you have to ensure that real teams do not develop the *best* architecture, but the most adequate. You have to avoid features that are implemented just because somebody *believes* they are needed. Technical teams have to think of themselves as service teams, delivering services to *their* customers, the domain teams. The big advantage of this strategy is that the architecture only contains what is required. This makes the architecture much easier to maintain and, as a side effect, cheaper. Additionally, it eliminates the oft-occurring social discrepancies between the technical and domain teams. One often gets the impression that those teams are working on different projects (not least from the way they talk about one another). Unfortunately, this impression is seldom wrong, and those teams have different objectives. Where technical teams' objective is to make use of a specific technology and develop perfect frameworks not requested by the domain teams, the domain teams' goal is to implement the domain, not caring if they can profit and learn from one another (or from the frameworks the technical teams provide).

But how do the technical service teams know which service is required and, more importantly, which requested service has the highest priority? The team has to come up with a strategy. Not every requirement from each and every domain team will be implemented, because certain requirements might contradict each other. Or, worse, implementing these requirements will cost so many resources that other teams will not be able to get their (more important) requirements done.

Therefore, like real customers, the domain teams have to speak with one voice. Retrospectives can serve as a forum for deciding on new or changed requirements since all teams are present (or at least represented) and the focus of the retrospective is the project's status and progress, anyway.[8] If one team states that it cannot proceed because it needs some special technical service, all teams can decide jointly if this is a requirement they support; if approved, the

---

[8]A retrospective is a reflective group meeting that is held at the end of a development cycle (see Chapter 4).

service will be a joint requirement for the technical service team. Otherwise, the requesting domain team has to implement the service on its own. These requirements are then scheduled in the same way the domain teams schedule their requirements. Thus, the technical service team schedules requirements with the highest priority first and does not schedule more than it can accomplish within the next development cycle. It might have to negotiate workload with the domain teams. At the beginning of the project, especially, the domain teams define many requirements for the technical service team, but at other times, there may be few requests, if, for example, the architecture can just be used as is. During "high season," you should ensure that the technical service team does not accept more work than it can accomplish. During "low season," you should ask the members of the technical service team to join the domain teams instead of implementing unnecessary additional features.

Requirements Channels, by Stefan Roock

In this project, we had to implement a system supporting multiple channels for different user groups, with various front-end technologies (desktop, Web, laptop). Our starting project team consisted of five people from the development company and two consultants. With seven people, it was a size typical for an agile project. We had all the Extreme Programming practices in place when the project had to scale up and accept additional manpower—mainly developers. The goal was to have about twenty-five people in the project.

When scaling up, we had to address the issue of project structure. It became clear that it would not be possible to integrate all these people in one large team in the project. Therefore, we decided to split the project up into teams. But, we asked ourselves, what are the criteria for the division of teams? Do we use the architecture as the structuring mechanism and assign each subsystem to a team? Or do we assign each requirements channel to a team? In the first case, each requirements channel had to talk with every team. In the second case, each team had to modify classes all over the system. Since the planning games seemed to be too complex in the former, we chose the latter.[9]

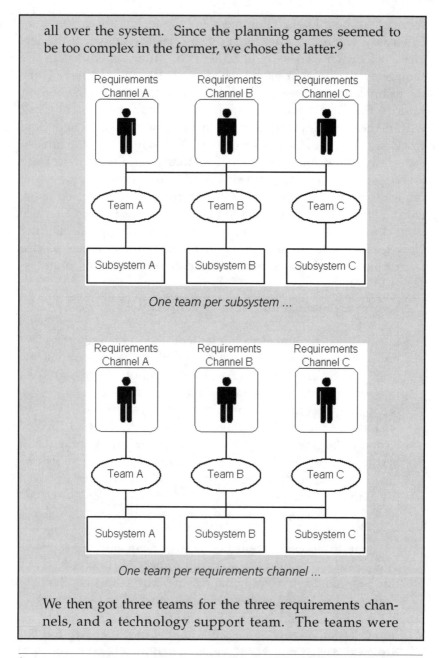

One team per subsystem ...

One team per requirements channel ...

We then got three teams for the three requirements channels, and a technology support team. The teams were

[9]The planning game is an Extreme Programming technique. The customers select and prioritize the tasks for the developers for the next development cycle and the developers estimate the effort for those tasks.

rather small (four people), which supported taking over responsibility.

One thing we learned was that reorganizing teams takes more time than we thought. When we changed the organizational structure, the developers needed several weeks to get used to the new structure and get up to their development speed again.

Because teams were not assigned to subsystems, every developer was able to modify every part of the system. This was no problem because the developers were able to master the code base (about twelve-hundred classes).

As time went by, additional developers joined the project and the code base grew. We ended up with about thirty developers with different programming skills. Now some developers weren't able to modify every part of the system without it breaking. Our first step was to tag core classes and the very complicated parts of the system as "expert code," which had to be modified by a so-called system expert.

That solved the problem, but it didn't seem to be a very smart solution since there was no way to guarantee that only system experts modify the crucial part of the system.

Currently, we are searching for better mechanisms for assigning code to teams. The main idea is to take the layering of subsystems into account. Some subsystems are specifically for a requirements channel and should be assigned to the relevant team. Other subsystems are relevant to several user groups and can't be assigned to one of the existing teams. These subsystems are assigned to a virtual "base subsystem" team, which is created on demand from the system experts sitting in the existing teams.

Team Roles

The idea is that a team must have members that possess all the required knowledge. In that sense, each team is a generalist in its domain. For instance, a domain team will be assembled by domain experts, graphical user interface developers, and database developers. But although the team consists of these different experts, those experts will not work solely in their field of speciality. Instead, the team members must take different roles. For example, it is rather typical for the database developer to learn from the graphical user interface specialist how to build the presentation, and to then contribute to the user interface development. Thus, the goal of having generalists rather than specialists on a team is attainable by spreading the available knowledge.

The goal of this approach is not egalitarianism of all team members. Distinct skills and experiences are still necessary for specific tasks. However, the goal is to avoid the general tendency toward thought monopolies and to spread knowledge and skills.

Additionally, each agile team also possesses the required administrative knowledge necessary to perform, for example, integration and configuration management. The person who takes this role concentrates mainly on issues based on internal team integration and configuration, but will also be this function's contact person for people external to the team. However, individual team members may have multiple roles: For instance, the person responsible for integration and configuration may be the domain expert, too.

It is very helpful to establish a team lead for every team. This person acts as a contact person for the whole team. Often, the team lead coordinates who will attend a specific meeting, such as a retrospective.

Team Jelling

Ideally, the whole project team pulls together, all team members communicate honestly and openly, and everybody has the same big picture in mind. As Tom DeMarco puts it, the team *jells*.[10] The pulling together must especially be supported so it becomes natural. In addition to the more formal aspects of project development, other, more enjoyable and motivational, tactics must be employed to keep your project on track:

---

[10]A team jells when it has a good chemistry, comparable to the chemistry good jelly has. For more on this subject, see Tom DeMarco, *The Deadline: A Novel About Project Management* (New York: Dorset House Publishing, 1997).

- **Food:** If you provide food, or just snacks—healthy or otherwise—the area where you place the food will soon become an extremely popular part of the office. And when groups of people are there, taking advantage of the free food, they will start talking. You might also want to make use of team lunches, although you should ensure that lunch time is also a break time that allows the team members to relax and recover from their work. On the other hand, breaking bread together always helps people get closer to one another.

- **Party:** Organize a party once in a while—after the delivery of a major release, for example. This does not have to be something big. It would be enough to serve some sandwiches and beverages for a couple of hours or so. This will help people who wouldn't otherwise have the chance to sit and talk to each other. Try to convince the company of the importance of such project parties, so it will approve them.

- **Recreation:** Organize some sort of recreational outing. It can be a sporting event, such as a volleyball match, or some other social event, such as bowling, go-cart racing, or something along those lines. Doing something as a group will help team members get to know each other, especially when people are asked to team up with someone they do not work with regularly. This will hopefully reinforce respect and acceptance among all. Ensure that everybody can participate in the event, taking into account team members' disabilities, for example.

- **Project identity:** Encourage the team members to cultivate a sense of project identity. Authors Mary Lynn Manns and Linda Rising stress the importance of having a group identity in *Fear Less: Patterns for Introducing New Ideas into Organizations*. They recommend a separate pattern, called *Group Identity*.[11] Special T-shirts, project-specific food and beverages, or even project-specific phrases and slogans help to develop a project culture. On one project, we even came up with a project cocktail. However, the project should not

---

[11]Mary Lynn Manns and Linda Rising, *Fear Less: Patterns for Introducing New Ideas into Organizations* (Boston: Addison-Wesley, 2004).

alienate itself from the outside; the group identity should help newcomers to identify themselves with the project.

- **Regeneration:** Ensure that project members have time to regenerate. Even when people are under pressure to deliver, make sure that they take their vacations and are not working overtime. A project is comparable to a marathon, not to a sprint.

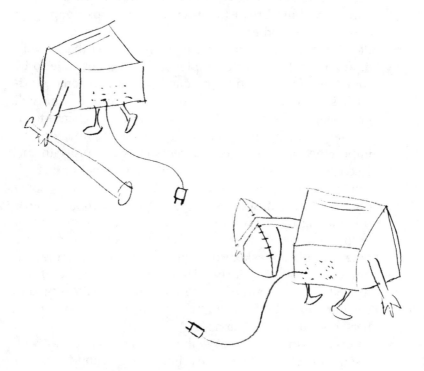

Regeneration ...

- **Communication of results:** You cannot overestimate how motivational it is for teams to have reports on the growth of the system or the customer's feedback. Therefore, make sure everybody knows about the project's progress.

All the strategies suggested (just a sample of the possibilities) reinforce communication and will ensure that your team members will get to know each other better and, more importantly, learn to respect one another. Try to ensure that members from different subteams interact with each other. For example, if you organize a sporting activity, you can request that each side contain no more than two people from the same subteam. It is astonishing how much this contributes to a sense of communal identity among team members, and this usually results in projects that run more smoothly.

Some strategies are not readily implemented in certain companies. For instance, organizing a party that needs temporal and financial support could be a problem. This is a sure sign that the importance of communication is still underestimated. You will need to convince the organization otherwise. It is worth the effort.

Interaction and Communication Structures

Communication is the most important factor in the success or failure of the whole project. Communication is difficult, even when only a few people are involved, but it gets exponentially more challenging as the number of people involved increases. When setting up a communication structure for a large team, you have to consider the following constraints:

- **Direct communication:** This the safest form of communication, and you know immediately if the receiver of your message understood what you said. However, the more people involved in a communication effort, the harder it is to get a message across. One reason for this is that there will not be enough time for everybody to actively participate in the conversation. Another reason is that participation may be dominated by a few extroverts, whereas all the introverts will accept the message out of discomfort with discussing anything in big groups.
- **Different sensory modalities:** Every person obtains information differently. Some people, known as visuals, learn most effectively by watching; auditories, by listening; and kinesthetics, through action.
- **Overdose on communication media:** There must be a law stating that as soon as a communication path works, it will be abused until it doesn't work anymore. For example, if

messages are exchanged via e-mail, you will read your e-mails and respond to them. However, once your inbox begins to overflow with new e-mails when you get to work each morning, either you will be very selective about which messages you read and respond to or you will ignore them all. This, of course, is bound to eventually result in your getting in trouble for not reading an e-mail that the sender assumed you read.

Changing communication channels …

Therefore, you should also be agile and flexible with communication. Use various modes of communication that address different persons differently, respecting their unique sensory modalities. Change the communication channels from time to time. That said, though, a manageable, average-sized agile project will always require direct communication.

Open-Plan Office

Ideally, the whole team sits in one room together with the customer. As Craig Larman writes in *Applying UML and Patterns*,

> Having a team on another floor of the same building has as much impact as if it were in a completely separate geographical location.[12]

However, in a large project with a team of a hundred or more members, space constraints make it difficult to have everyone in one office. Open-plan offices are valuable in both creating space and enhancing communication. They can be created by removing cubicles or by positioning the cubicles around teams rather than individuals. Open-plan offices can sometimes accommodate forty to fifty people. So, if you can have two or three such offices next to each other, project members will be sitting in quarters that are as close as possible.

Open-Plan Offices, by Nicolai M. Josuttis

At the start of my professional life, open-plan offices had a bad reputation. They represented the idea of treating human beings like machines, which can be located close together in a big hall to save money on walls. And in fact, in a work environment that assigns each employee a stupid and almost communication-free task, there is a lot to be said against putting large groups of people together in a huge room, like in a laying battery or factory floor—especially if phone calls annoy one's neighbors, and one has to fight tediously for each square meter of space.

After my first large agile project, however, I began to look at open-plan offices from a different perspective. The situation changes tremendously when the job focuses on

---

[12]Craig Larman, *Applying UML and Patterns: An Introduction to Object-Oriented Analysis and Design* (Englewood Cliffs, N.J.: Prentice Hall, 1998), p. 448.

teamwork that enables several people to create something together. All of a sudden, moving to another room is painful. All of a sudden, it is important to know what your colleagues are working on. All of a sudden, it is important to work *together*, collaboratively and physically. The value of this kind of communication can't be overestimated.

However, this does not mean that it is best for an agile project to pack all project members together in a dreary open-plan office. It is important to be able to have a meeting without disturbing others. Adequately sound-proofed meeting rooms are a necessity. Also, individual workplaces are important for people who need a quiet place to think, design, or make a phone call. Glass works well for this purpose: Vitreous meeting rooms, individual vitreous workplaces, or vitreous walls between teams allow the necessary transparency without raising the noise to a degree that disables serious work.

In a sense, an agile workplace is an intelligent mix of everything, which is again typical for agility in general.

Always ensure that the individual subteams can sit together, even inside an open-plan office. Although this might seem like common sense, it is not as common a situation as it should be. Again, whatever your constraints, the distance between team members has a major influence on the success or failure of your project. Be aware that this distance does not necessarily have to be physical. For instance, if certain team members listen to music through headphones while they work, the headphones establish a distance between them and their peers. The least you can do is to make it possible for all members of the team to be on the same floor or, at the very least, in the same building. But everything that improves the seating situation pays off during development time.

Some people argue that the noise levels are too high in open-plan offices. This is not usually an issue. Mainly because everybody is concentrating too intensely on his or her work to be disturbed by the conversations of others. However, you may have some individuals in the team with particularly loud voices. In that case, you should ask them to lower their voice. If this is not possible, you should consider locating said individuals to a place where they will not disturb their peers. But this is a highly unlikely situation. As I said earlier, in my experience, the noise level on projects is almost always acceptable, and the advantages of the close proximity of team members far outweigh those of having a quiet environment.

Flexible Workplace

Nowadays, some companies do not support assigned office space. Instead, they use a system known as *flexible workplace* (also known as floating desks or desk-sharing), where people just sit wherever they find some space. Team members either use cell phones or have calls transferred to wherever they are sitting on a particular day. Typically, filing cabinets are mobile, so team members can have all their papers with them at all times. The underlying idea of the flexible workplace is that it requires less space than a more traditional, assigned-space system. The logic being that, on any given day, certain employees will not be in the office: People call in sick, take vacations, make on-site visits to customers, and so on. Utilizing flexible workplaces, then, is a very efficient way to use office space and to save money on workplaces.

However, the catch is that you will never know, for sure, where to find a specific person, and this is a communication problem. Another problem is that at certain times (during the less popular vacation months, for example), some people may spend their day wandering around looking for an empty space to sit.

Remarkably, this problem sometimes becomes known outside of flexible workplaces. One time, in a taxi I was taking from the airport to a customer's office, the driver asked if she should speed up to make sure I would have a place to sit at the office. (It turned out not to be necessary, since we had plenty of time to spare; it was just eight o'clock in the morning.)

Another risk that teams utilizing flexible workplaces face is that people may get to work late and not be able to sit with the other members of their team. At that point, flexible workplaces are not very beneficial.

If you cannot avoid a flexible workplace arrangement, try to establish an acceptable working environment, for example by defining (flexible) team zones within the constraints of your office's seating arrangement. Be aware that in your attempts to do so, you might get in trouble with the "office police." In such a case, you have to fight this out, because as mentioned earlier, the importance of efficient communication cannot be valued high enough.

Flexible workplaces create an infrastructure that allows people and teams to solve communication problems by relocating easily. However, if your company has the philosophy that every associate should have the same desk over many years, you might discover unbelievable resistance when transitioning to flexible workplaces to better support the project.

Encouraging Communication

The real difficulty of working with a large team is looking for ways to ensure efficient communication. I have found that the following steps are valuable in setting up a communication structure:

- All project members should sit as close together as possible without crowding each other.
- The retrospectives performed after each iteration and release cycle serve as a forum for direct communication. Typically, the topics of optimizing the space and improving direct communication for the daily work will be discussed regularly until they are resolved.
- Regularly scheduled meetings for *all* project members are essential. Such meetings are primarily a mode of information transfer. In my experience, too many people attend these meetings for there to be any effective feedback or extensive discussions, but they work well for one-directional information transfer. Therefore, every project member should have the possibility to contribute—in the form of a lecture about a specific topic, for example. It is a good idea to announce the contents of the contributions in advance.
- Provide a *wiki* on the intranet, not only as a means for documentation, but as a means for communication.[13]

---

[13]The term "wiki" is Hawaiian for "quick," which in this context represents the ability to make quick changes. For more information on wikis, see Leuf and Cunningham, op. cit.

The philosophy of a wiki is to allow all kinds of discussion on the Web. Everybody has the right to make changes to the Websites. This is possible through editable HTML pages. The wiki Web only knows collective ownership, so everybody has the same responsibility for the contents. This helps to establish a community of trust. Furthermore, no deep knowledge of HTML is required to contribute to the wiki Web. You can even contribute by writing plain text. If the wiki Web is also used to document the project, you can be sure that this will always be a good source of project documentation.

- Establish different e-mail distribution lists that allow you to address everyone involved in the project, as well as specific groups of people.

Communication Team

Be warned, however, that even making use of these different channels will not eliminate your communication problems. Another very effective way of improving your team's communication is to establish a separate (virtual) communication team. Depending on the size of your team, the communication team could consist of just one person. The communication team is responsible for visiting all the teams regularly, obtaining feedback, and discovering deficiencies and (potential) problems, possibly solving them immediately. It is important for the team to proactively approach the project members. You will recognize problems sooner this way than by waiting until they escalate or are reported officially. Typical topics and tasks of the communication team are

- **Unified project culture:** The goal is to establish a common culture regarding guidelines, tests, patterns, and the like.
- **Refactoring:** Uncovering sources for refactoring not only improves the quality of the code but also provides learning opportunities for everybody.
- **Common understanding:** The communication team needs to ensure that all information, decisions, and announcements are understood by all the teams.
- **Problem discovery and treatment:** Problems should be detected and, at best, solved immediately and in a simple

manner. The communication team has the advantage of having an overview of all the teams. This way, the communication team can establish contact or point to solutions other teams might have found. If several teams have the same problems, general strategies are required for solving these problems (extending/adapting the framework, or providing patterns for the solution). Furthermore, the communication team suggests ways that the process could help overcome or eliminate the encountered problems.

The members of the communication team should never act as supervisors or controllers, but instead more like a team of ombudsmen. These ombudsmen should be sensitive to the hopes and fears of the individual team members and should collect suggestions for process improvements. For example, ensuring that the team members understand the decisions enables them to either accept the decisions or to suggest a solution that supports them better.

It is very important that the members of the communication team have a good overview, are well-trusted people with good communication skills, and are widely accepted and respected by the rest of the project team. These people should be able to take matters into their own hands, able to manage the project as a whole, but also have good connections to the individual persons. In smaller teams, the communication team will consist of just one person, with tasks that cross boundaries—running reviews, retrospectives, coaching the process, and so on. In larger teams (with more than fifty people), this will always be a full-time job for one or even more persons.

You will rarely find a project organization that is aware of the necessity of this role. This makes it difficult to establish this position. I often call these people communication managers or, simply, *catalysts*. Ideally, as Tom DeMarco and Timothy Lister write, these are people whose mere presence is enough to ensure that a project runs smoothly.[14]

---

[14]Tom DeMarco and Timothy Lister, *Peopleware: Productive Projects and Teams,* 2nd ed. (New York: Dorset House Publishing, 1999).

Trouble-Shooting

Sometimes, you need to act quickly—for example, if one of the teams is completely under stress, one team stops talking to another team, or two teams start continuously blaming one another and are not able to work together anymore. In such situations, you face two difficult tasks: One is to look at the problem and see exactly what kind it is, and the other is to solve the problem.

Smells …

The first task is more difficult, because it depends a lot on the team's culture. Here are some typical problem signs:

- **Cynicism and sarcasm:** Humor is a sign that everything is right on track and that people are having fun doing their jobs. But if the humor turns into sarcasm, this is a clear sign that the team does not jell and does not believe in what it is doing.
- **Blame:** This sign is much more obvious and therefore easier to tackle. The teams or people blaming each other usually have problems respecting and understanding each other. Sometimes, though, blame can be a sign of difficulty in communicating.

- **Lack of feedback:** This is often a sign that the people have given up. They do not believe in reaching the goal and they do not believe that anybody has an interest in their opinion or in their effort.

Whatever the reason is, you can neither accept nor ignore the situation. All these circumstances will slow down the project's progress significantly. Therefore,

- If a team is under stress and complains that it cannot get its work done because there are too many meetings or its time is spent supporting other teams, protect the team for a couple of hours each day by arranging *quiet times*. It might be necessary to arrange an office-wide quiet time, either temporarily or permanently. For more on quiet times, see Alistair Cockburn's *Agile Software Development,* in which the author suggests defining the period between 10 A.M. and 12 P.M. as quiet time, during which no phone calls or meetings are allowed.[15]

   If instituting quiet time is not sufficient to bring the team back on track, a more rigorous approach is required: Instead of quiet hours, make sure the team will get one or two quiet weeks, with one or two hours of each day as "regular office hours," so that team members can still process incoming requests.

   The most extreme solution is to send the team to a closed meeting for a couple of days. In addition to being extreme, this solution is the most effective and probably the most expensive. Closed meetings are often used in other circumstances: for example, if the team does not jell or has to consider different kinds of solutions. They are most often used as an environment for the project kick-off (for making teams jell) and for the project postmortems.[16]

   Quiet times have a trade-off: They can also lead to a complete lack of communication and should therefore be carefully balanced.

---

[15]Alistair Cockburn, *Agile Software Development* (Reading, Mass.: Addison-Wesley, 2002).

[16]For more on postmortems, see Norman L. Kerth, *Project Retrospectives: A Handbook for Team Reviews* (New York: Dorset House Publishing, 2001).

- If two teams stop talking or working together efficiently, locate them next to each other. This way, each team will recognize why the other acts as it does, and they will start to respect one another.

  Another strategy is to set up a voluntary exchange program among teams, so that each member switches place with a member of another team.[17]

  Both strategies help to improve the understanding between the teams.

- If a meeting culture evolves where people have to spend more time in meetings than they do working, and if people start complaining about unnecessary meetings, challenge the reason for holding each of the established meetings, especially all regular meetings. Furthermore, you should determine which participants are not required to attend in order for the meeting to be a success.

  Generally, you should introduce the "law of the two feet," as described by the Open Space Technology: Anybody who feels that the meeting is a waste of time is allowed to leave. This might require some sensitivity from the organizer of the meeting: If a participant does not contribute, he or she should be politely invited, outside the meeting, to contribute to the project's success.

  Introducing quiet times is another approach to overcoming the meeting culture.

- Finally, you can at the beginning of each meeting ask one of the participants to excuse himself or herself from the meeting to do something more important (this was first suggested by Tom DeMarco, in *The Deadline*).[18] Take care that a different person is excused each time, and is not the most junior person.

- If a team is not very well integrated—for example, if it is often not well-informed or is often blamed by other teams for incidents that stemmed from a lack of information— then locate food in the team's area. Normally, it is only a matter of hours before other teams find themselves in the

---

[17]Thanks to Mike Cohn for sharing this approach.

[18]DeMarco, op. cit.

food area and the communication or information flow is reestablished naturally.

Virtual Teams

According to researchers in the area of work life, virtual teams will become the norm in the future. Fewer and fewer real teams will physically come together to work on a project, and more and more teams will be assembled over the Internet. This has a lot of advantages:

- Each individual project member is responsible for his or her own work space and environment. Although sometimes the client will provide the equipment, most often the individual project member will have to use his or her own hardware. This saves the client a lot of money.
- You have much better access to different skills. You are not limited to people from your region or your company.
- You are not responsible for the team in the long run. You only have to pay it for as long as it works for you. You are under no obligation to find its members their next job.
- If the team is distributed all over the world, another advantage is that at any hour, at least one team member is most likely working on the project. There is hardly any project off-time.

The main problem with virtual teams is that they lack the most efficient mode of communication—direct communication. As Erran Carmel and Ritu Agarwal write,

> Distance negatively affects communication, which in turn reduces coordination effectiveness.[19]

In virtual teams, the problem isn't just communication with the customer; it's also communication inside the team. It's very difficult for a virtual team to get a common understanding and to pull together.

---

[19]Erran Carmel and Ritu Agarwal, "Tactical Approaches for Alleviating Distance in Global Software Development," *IEEE Software*, Vol. 18, No. 2 (March/April, 2001), p. 23.

Distributed Teams

Large teams are always distributed in one way or another, just because they are too large to contain in one room. However, distributed development is somewhat more extreme, in that the project members are distributed over several sites and, as the term suggests, the project itself is developed in a dispersed manner. Sometimes, you might find a single team spread over several sites; other times, several teams are each located at a different site. Outsourcing is one example of a distributed team, as I discuss in Chapter 6.

One problem in this setting is ensuring that everybody on the team pulls together. On projects like this, you will often find that people blame one another, mainly because they do not know each other and therefore do not trust each other. Also, technical topics like version and configuration management are even more complicated in distributed teams. Of course, there are tools that can help manage these more complex areas of development, but they do not make up for the inconvenience and problems caused by distributed development.

If you must have distributed teams, the Internet is likely to be your main form of communication (e-mail, wiki Web, chat rooms), and video conferencing is also a good way to communicate. However, be sure that people working out of different locations are able to meet with each other, at least occasionally. Communicating through the Internet will only work efficiently if people know and trust each other—and there is no better way of building trust than through personal contact.

Distributed Teams, by David Hussman

Most agile practices ask project members to keep communication channels open and filled with honest dialogue, without regard to the message content. Nowhere is this more important than on an agile project with distributed teams. Along with the usual technical challenges of distributed development, agile development brings even more challenges, mostly aimed at those outside the development teams.

Project managers, coaches, and customers need to be vigilant when it comes to listening to and addressing the developer's concerns; tracking successes and failures; the way in which story content is gathered, organized, and presented; and the consistency of the process and the development environments.[20] With distributed teams, the need to embrace change and make the necessary corrections to the direction of the project sooner than later is even greater. Just as the last car of a long train starts moving long after the first, so too does change take longer to move through the distributed teams.

The following list of best and worst practices might help those outside the development group find and address needed changes before the project strays too far from the correct path. Many of the listed items apply to any scaled, agile project, but their importance is heightened when the development teams are distributed:

Best Practices

- **Customer agility:** Ensure that customer teams can make any necessary changes by keeping the ratio of customers to developers as low as possible (one customer to three or fewer developers; the larger the project, the smaller the ratio). The ability of the customer team to react and change direction can be difficult when stories cross team boundaries and teams struggle to bring portions of a software solution to fruition. For example, if five people are writing a book together, with each person working on a different chapter, the lucidity and cohesiveness of the

---

[20]Extreme Programming uses the term "stories" for requirements, which are defined by the customer for a release cycle. User stories are comparable to use-cases in UML.

book is proportional to the amount of time the authors spend discussing the book with each other.

- **Group speak:** The more often that project managers, coaches, and trackers discuss planning and development issues, the better. Although this discussion can take place over e-mail, at a wiki site, and through non-verbal channels, ensure that at some point there are conference calls or video conferences. If possible, have a different team lead the discussion on every call (this helps all involved to embrace the project). Also, as teams grow and change, each group starts to form its own view of the project picture. Sharing your team's lingo with other teams can aid in maintaining a common view and provide cross-team insight.

- **Common acceptance:** If possible, ensure that each team is building and testing against a common set of hardware and software (if this is not possible, discuss the environmental differences regularly). The closer the environments, the better the level of acceptance testing. Try utilizing a common acceptance testing strategy, and whenever possible share the data sets used for testing. Try to start automated acceptance testing early, and run the tests as often as possible.

- **Developer rotation:** Often times, teams in the same building feel as disconnected from each other as teams separated by states or countries. If possible, move players from team to team. If the players cannot co-locate, explore the notion of rotating the work done by the teams instead of the team members themselves. This may seem like an unrealistic suggestion, but it may be a way to help maintain a healthy project whose members have a holistic perspective.

Worst Practices

- **Technical stratification:** It is often a natural fit for distributed teams to work on subjects that they are familiar with (this is often why distributed teams are brought into a project). If at all possible, avoid splitting development tasks across technical boundaries. Try instead to plan and develop toward functional goals and subdivide the work from that perspective (this will avoid the classic producer-consumer relationship between teams, where one team has finished all its work and is left with nothing to do).

- **Failure to communicate mock implementations:** As teams may not have everything that they need in order to complete a particular feature, they may choose to mock or stub-out temporary solutions.[21] This is fine (and, if everyone is using the same code base and acceptance tests, it can be quite clear), but make sure that the interfaces to the mocks or stubs are agreed upon by all.

- **Loss of iteration synchronization:** In most cases, it is best to keep all teams on similar iteration boundaries. It may be that the teams (and more importantly, those in charge of the planning) find a steady state with varied iteration boundaries. In either case, ensure that the iteration synchronization is as constant as possible. Again, as with scaled, agile projects, if a team has an iteration schedule slip, even of just a couple

---

[21]Mock and stub objects allow you to test partial solutions by simulating the missing code.

of days, planning issues may arise that are best dealt with by moving the incomplete features to the next iteration. The difference may seem small, but the consistency will benefit the project plan.

Conclusion

Distributed teams using agile practices face many of the same problems that subteams face when agile projects scale to large numbers. The need for vigilant and constant communication is exacerbated. Small issues can quickly grow large or span several iterations if not known to all team members. One team's frustration can affect other teams without it even knowing it. Strive to keep process, schedules, and environments constant, and when they change (as we know they will), notify all involved as soon as possible. The more that can be shared between teams (source code, data, and so on), the easier this task will be. Ensure that planners listen to the developers, and help them listen to one another.

Open Source

Open source projects are well-functioning examples of virtual teams. Possible reasons for their success are

- All the team members are very idealistic. There is no need to motivate them or try to ensure that they identify themselves with the project. This all comes naturally.
- Everybody feels responsible for the whole project and takes this responsibility very seriously.
- There is a broad community that provides immediate feedback. This feedback is what drives the whole project. There is no difference in the value of feedback whether it comes from peers or from users.
- Everybody who contributes to the project takes pride in his or her work.

The main underlying principle of open source projects, and the reason for their success, is the gift economy (the culture of giving away capacity and information). This means that everybody working on an open source project is doing so voluntarily. A lot can be learned from this approach, especially for use on commercial projects.

Mary Poppendieck once reported that a new project manager asked her for advice on becoming a successful team leader. She asked him if he had ever led a team of volunteers (of any sort). He replied that he had been a successful choir leader. Poppendieck continues,

> I suggested that if he used the same techniques with his project team that he did with his choir, he would be a successful project manager. He said it was the best advice he ever received, and he blossomed as a project manager.[22]

Open Source, by Dierk König

The open source movement derives its name from the practice of sharing the source code of a valuable product among an arbitrary number of developers. This so-called collective code ownership means that the code belongs to all these developers. They are entitled to change it and are responsible for the final result.

In the context of this book, open source projects may be of interest because they share properties of both large and agile projects. They make use of agile practices while suffering from the same problems that large projects have in regard to team distribution.

I'm not so bold as to claim that open source produces better results in general. Sure, lots of open source products are widely known for having excellent quality with zero costs to the user. But I'm the first to admit that there are also numerous sloppy projects out there that will never produce anything useful. However, maybe we can take something from the successful ones!

---

[22]Mary Poppendieck, personal e-mail correspondence on the gift economy.

Distribution

It is evident that the physical co-location of all of the contributors to an open source project is impossible. However, we have observed that members of the core editing team of an open source project sometimes get together to tackle a special issue, often sacrificing personal time and money. The collaboration then looks like an Extreme Programming pair programming session.[23]

Even the users of open source software hold events so they can get together and share their experience. The Eclipse Code Camp is one example.[24]

If the open source people put so much effort into overcoming the obstacle of distribution, can we—in paid time—go upstairs to pair up with the database guy?

Idiosyncrasies

An open source contributor is not forced into anything. If you do not like anything about the project (the setup, the code style, the technology, the people, and so on), you can leave at any time or even *fork* (make a new project based on the old one).

This, and the fact that a lot of people write contributions in their spare time, leads to a project staff that likes the applied work style, or at the very least accepts it. The number of complaints is noticeably small.

One could claim that open source projects are not limited in time, scope, or resources, and therefore do not need the measures of control that are applied to in-house projects. This is not really true. Running an open source project in your spare time, knowing you have

---

[23]Extreme Programming requires developers to write productive code in pairs. Thus, a continuous review takes place throughout the development by two developers working together.

[24]Developers of the Eclipse development environment meet occasionally in so-called code camps to exchange experiences and develop the product further (see http://www.eclipse.org/).

only a few hours a week to work on it, makes you think hard about what to implement next.

Open source is opportunity-driven. Whoever needs a feature the most will implement it and submit the contribution. Nothing is produced for the shelf. Contributors undertake their tasks without anyone telling them to.

Developers know that their code will be read, literally, hundreds of times. This is motivation enough for them to achieve high code quality, and it is a good opportunity to show off their professional expertise.

Now, without any imposed order, programmers do what they think is appropriate; surprisingly, this does not result in total chaos, but rather in automated testing techniques, stable and frequent builds, ubiquitous version control, flexible architectures, and self-documenting code. Most astonishing is that these programmers manage to achieve something that most organizations do not: mutual respect among team members.

Architecture

Open source projects typically do not start with an up-front architecture (Eclipse may be an exception), but they always have one in the end. The opportunity-driven nature and the resource constraints of open source force contributors to practice reuse. This is especially apparent in the Jakarta project family.[25] Every project is built on other projects, which were built on projects that came before them, and so on.

The new challenge is to manage project dependencies, a well-known problem that most big organizations struggle with. Open source offers an easy yet powerful alternative: Let the user decide.

Another idiosyncrasy of open source architectures is the focus on extension points and pluggability. JUnit,

---

[25]For Jakarta, see http://jakarta.apache.org/.

ANT, and Eclipse are perfect examples of this approach.[26]

Just think of the effect that applying the principles of open source software would have on your corporate IT projects.

Project Structure

In open source projects, you typically see a core team of editors with write access to the repository. The requirements for becoming an editor differ on every project. Some do not have any restrictions, while others only grant write access to contributors that consistently submit quality work. Some projects have a fixed group of editors.

The core team decides whether contributions from the outside get incorporated or rejected.

Communication channels are highly self-organized. The flow of information typically takes place on mailing lists.

Project Setup

For open source projects, having a self-contained build is absolutely crucial. It is no wonder that open source projects were the pioneers of build automation. The same holds true for the use of versioning systems, nightly builds, and automated self-testing.

As the source code is highly visible, a new degree of rigor is applied to the end result. The source code is subject to excruciating review and refinement. Its compliance to every standard in use will be checked for all platforms the community uses. The contributor has total control over how to achieve this result. Assessing results rigorously but giving developers freedom to use their own work style is a strong agile move that large projects can follow as well.

---

[26]For JUnit, see http://www.junit.org/; for ANT, see http://www.ant.org/.

Documentation

Typically, in open source software there is not a lot of external documentation. The code must speak for itself. Although it may seem unusual, this strategy works well on open source projects, where the code, especially the test code, must reveal its intention.

Successful projects are often accompanied by articles and even books. The usage documentation that comes with the distribution typically contains only very basic help for the beginner.

It appears that any necessary external documentation gets written on request. For example, in Canoo WebTest, we had a fairly complicated security use-case.[27] A user volunteered to write the documentation for this, provided that someone helped him figure out what to do.

The result seems to be a good balance between the two extremes of lacking all the necessary information and having excessive documentation in which the important information is hidden among pages and pages of unnecessary text.

Planning

Frankly, there is no long-term planning whatsoever. There are exceptions, but for most open source projects, there is only a little short-term planning. The reason for this is to save the developers unnecessary work by not prescribing long-term directions of any greater detail than a common vision. Directions are derived solely from user feedback.

The most challenging part of adopting open source strategies in corporate IT projects may be trusting in the evolution and refinement of a complex adaptive system that is beyond managerial control.

---

[27]For WebTest, see http://www.webtest.canoo.com/.

Summary

You should never underestimate the value of face-to-face communication, especially with large and distributed teams. You should do everything you can to provide as many opportunities as possible for direct communication. Direct communication, together with transparency, helps to build trust, both inside the team and between the team and the outside world. If team members trust one another, they will not fear taking up responsibility.

A tool like the wiki Web will help you build trust by empowering everybody through shared ownership. In doing so, such tools change the flow of communication from control-driven to collaborative-driven.

When building subteams, you should ensure that the skills within each subteam are mixed. Furthermore, the technical service teams should serve the domain teams. If so desired, they can also be established as virtual teams.

Last but not least, allow the team to have fun. This not only helps teams jell, but more importantly, it also makes the work environment a pleasant one, which will make everybody want to work and succeed with the team. Consider the values of the gift economy the way the open source does; this will also help make work much more enjoyable.

4

AGILITY AND THE PROCESS

You should neither rant,
nor condemn,
but strive,
to improve the bad you see.
        —Leo N. Tolstoy

Agile processes were originally developed to support small teams. In order to make them work for large teams, they have to be modified. You need to exaggerate or institutionalize some of the characteristics of the process so that the values and underlying principles of the Agile Manifesto are still upheld. Some of these principles need special support in large teams, because they do not work as naturally in large teams as in small ones. For example, you have to take great care that project members still interact and communicate, despite working in different subteams.

In this chapter, we look at the criteria for creating and establishing an agile process for a large team. This chapter does not focus on the detailed process that every subteam will use, because each subteam is a small team and is therefore able to take advantage of all kinds of agile processes. Thus, some subteams might follow Extreme Programming while others might prefer to use Scrum, for example. Instead, we concentrate on the process specialties that ensure that all the subteams pull together and remain agile in their activities.

First, we discuss how to ensure that everybody on the team understands the project's objective. Then, we discuss the importance of providing feedback. After this, we dive into the construction of development cycles and the interdependencies between releases, iterations, and time-boxes. This is followed by a look at how we plan, integrate, and reflect on the (intended) outcomes of such a release cycle. With this knowledge in mind, we examine how we can start establishing such an agile process within a large team and how this impacts the corporate culture.

Defining the Objectives

You can try this yourself: Interview the members of a large team and ask them how they know when they are done. You will be surprised at how few of those asked will be able to give you an answer that involves fulfilling the objectives of the project rather than of the deadline. This is because software team members are always extremely aware of their deadline, but not of their project's mission.

Why are people so unclear about their objectives? Because the team is so large, the developers do not feel they have to be aware of the objectives, thinking that somebody higher up the hierarchy will know. Unsurprisingly, those higher up in the hierarchy often do not have a clear and joint understanding about the objectives either. They just go about doing their little part without being aware of—or rather, caring about—the whole.

Therefore, make sure that the common objective, defined in the mission statement, is known by all project members. Otherwise, the risk will be high that project members will not pull together and will act instead as if they are working on different projects—not toward a common goal.

In trying to motivate all involved to work toward this common goal, you might encounter a problem similar to one I encountered—only once, luckily: The person assigned to be the project manager was given that position for this project only. It was understood that after the project was over, he would return to his usual position, a bit lower in the hierarchy. Well, you can probably imagine what happened: The project manager was not particularly motivated to finish the project. There wasn't a lot I could do in such a situation except to ignore the hierarchy and discuss the matter with the project manager's superiors.

Providing Feedback

Interaction and communication serve as the focal point of all agile processes, but making the switch to an agile approach requires changes in other areas, too. One is the transition from linear (waterfall) development to iterative, incremental development. This has a massive impact on the usual development practices. For example, the iterative, incremental approach does not allow software to be developed in the dark, as is sometimes done in linear development: After clarifying the requirements, the project team "hides" in the development zone, without any contact with the outside world (especially not the customer). And only when the deadline arises are they asked to show the application. Before the deadline, nobody expects a working system to exist.

Feedback loop ...

In an agile process, everybody—from the development team itself to the customer—is invited to give feedback on the system, to help improve it. But this is not the only benefit of early and frequent feedback. Feedback also helps teams

- build reliability and trust between the customer and the project
- increase the team's confidence in its work, which will lead to motivation and job satisfaction
- establish a routine for development, integration, and even production and maintenance
- evaluate the architecture
- get a better understanding of the domain and the requirements
- protect the customer from complete failure by providing a system that is usable and covers all the functions requested

Therefore, ensure that you have a running system as early as possible, as it will allow you to benefit from continuous feedback.

Short Development Cycles, Iterations, and Time-Boxing

A development cycle is defined by a time-box (see Chapter 2) and results in a predetermined outcome. The length of the time-box depends on the state of the project, among other things.

A *release cycle* is a development cycle with a determined outcome, called a release (of software). Sometimes, teams like to distinguish between internal and external releases. Both should result in working, usable software. But only the external release is intended for delivery to the customer, whereas the internal release is just that—internal—and stays inside the company. But even an internal release has to go through all the acceptance tests that the external release goes through, so there is no real difference in quality or functionality between an external and internal release. The internal release usually only includes the working software; it rarely consists of other required artifacts, such as documentation.

The release cycles are again divided into other development cycles, so-called *iterations*, each of which result also in determined (partial) outcomes. The defined outcomes of an iteration are directly related to the planned results of the release cycle, because between release and iteration exists a whole-part relation. Sometimes, the desired outcome of an iteration is not achieved, and several iterations are required for it to be reached. While this is okay on the scale of an iteration, it is important that at the end of a release cycle, the desired results have been achieved and do not span over several releases. That way, we can always present the current release as a closed system to the customer.

If the team is already used to iterative, incremental development, you should not encounter too many obstacles when focusing on this topic. But if the team is used to linear development, the change will probably be seen as very drastic. Beware that sometimes people claim to practice iterative, incremental development without actually doing so. To make this obvious, here is an admittedly exaggerated example: Imagine we have a project scheduled for two years, on which we are going to use an iterative approach. The idea is for the project to be developed in *one* iteration, resulting in *one*—the final—release (which is the only increment). Even if an iteration lasts half a year, this does not mean an iterative, incremental process has been established. Only when setting up very short development cycles will you benefit from an iterative, incremental approach.

Although you may have heard otherwise, the larger the team is, the more important *short* cycles are. The reason is simple—if a large team takes the completely wrong course for the entirety of its three-month development cycle, the cost of correcting the course will be enormous. And even if the team took the correct course, it wouldn't benefit from the frequent feedback that is possible with short development cycles. Therefore, to have a good chance of successful delivery, you have to implement extremely short cycles from the beginning. For normal-sized teams, agile processes recommend a release cycle of one to three months, with iterations expanding to one to four weeks. By normal-sized, I mean teams of around fifteen people (sometimes less); in agile development, teams are quite a bit smaller than in other schools of development. Even with "large" agile teams, one assumes there are fewer than fifty members.

In order to make it easier for your (really) large team to correct its course, make sure the release cycles and iterations are at the lower end of, or are even shorter than, the recommendations stated above. In my experience, for a team with a hundred or more developers, it is best to start with release cycles of three to four weeks, with one-week iterations. As stated earlier, the time frames for the iterations and releases are time-boxed, so their length is fixed. There is no way of prolonging or shortening the time frame. If a release cycle lasts four weeks, only the functionality that has been completed during that time will be considered as delivered in that release.

On some of the projects I have worked on, discussions arose as to whether certain things were or were not completed or delivered. Some teams occasionally argued that an unfinished task of theirs was almost done and should therefore have been considered completed. In mediating these discussions, I used an approach I learned from Rob Mee and Joshua Kerievsky: I made a project-wide task list with three check boxes, labeled "started," "finished," and "accepted," next to each task. Thus, only if a task had been accepted was it considered completed. The discrimination between finished and accepted makes it obvious that a task counts only as completed (or delivered) if it has been accepted (and integrated). The acceptance is verified by the acceptance tests. This method works best if the task list is placed in a prominent position—either on a whiteboard or flip chart near the team's primary work space, or on the wiki Web. This way, everybody can see what the team is currently working on. This task list is also useful in steering the project, because it makes visual how realistic the team's estimations are.

At the beginning of a project, it is especially more important to keep cycles short because this early phase is when corrections will be required most frequently. This recommendation is debatable. Some people suggest the opposite: scheduling long cycles at the beginning of the development, to aid in setting everything up. My take is that you can split the set-up into smaller tasks in order to receive early feedback. Plus, you will probably have the steepest learning curve at the beginning of the project, and since we learn from our failures, it makes sense to make most of the (rather inevitable) failures at the beginning of a project, with its accelerated learning curve. This is why you should regard the first development cycle as an investment. Although it will be performed and planned like all those to follow, its main purpose is to allow you to learn from your mistakes.

Make sure that everybody understands that it is okay to make mistakes. Spreading this message early on helps also to establish a culture of failure (see Chapter 6), which will enable everyone to learn from failures.

Be sure, however, to make it known that the first cycle has to be executed in the same way as all the rest. In one project, a team argued that it would not be able to start immediately on the first iteration. The team's main arguments dealt with its impression that it would need to set up everything before it would be able to start doing real work. However, I asked the team members to plan, estimate, prioritize, and schedule these "set-ups" just as they would with any other task. This was important because a team needs to practice planning and performing iterations.

On a different project, I had a similar discussion, but this time it was after the first development cycle. Here, the team argued that this development cycle should be prolonged because so much time was lost setting things up. I explained to the team that there will always be problems and setbacks, but development cycles are fixed, and that in the future it would have to take this into account when scheduling its tasks.

Occasionally, invite all project members, including project management, to question the current time frame of the time-box. This is all part of a typical reflection, normally held as a retrospective at the end of the development cycle. For example, after the starting phase, you might want to check if the time frames for the subsequent development cycles should be altered. But be sure not to question these time frames too often. Doing so will disturb the rhythm of the project. However, it could be possible that after the starting phase, the team may want to change the process in a way that will increase the time needed to complete the following cycles.

In my experience, though, people usually want to stick to the short cycles, probably because they are used to their rhythm. Starting with really short cycles seems to help implement the change to an agile process. If the cycles are short, it is very difficult for the whole team to fall back into its old habits—it feels as if *everything* has changed; the altered environment makes it difficult to cultivate old habits. Sometimes, it is easier to implement a change if you exaggerate the implementation. This exaggeration is also called *shock-effect*—people are so shocked by the tremendous change that they are more or less forced to adapt to this change, and the shock eliminates their fear of change.

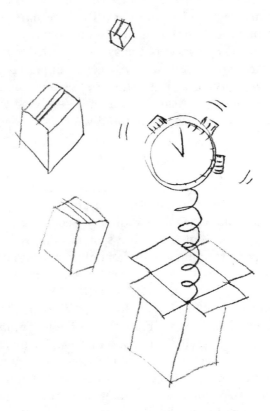

Time-box …

Of course, this is definitely not the best way to introduce every kind of change (I discuss introducing change in more detail later in this chapter). It's quite possible that some changes won't work out for a specific team at all, or have to be introduced very carefully. However, short cycles are best introduced suddenly and are almost impossible to do smoothly. If you shorten the cycles gradually, you will miss out on all the aforementioned benefits, most importantly, the *early* feedback, and it will be much more difficult for the team to get used to the rhythm. And, as we discussed above, early feedback is important, especially at the beginning, to help permanently correct the course.

If you deliver to your customer regularly, and on time, the customer will gain more and more confidence in the team and in the system. Often, though, the customer will be used to working with teams that are required to deliver all functionality in the first release. On previous projects, such customers may have found that when changes to any aspect of the system's functionality are postponed to a later release, at least two years will pass before the feature is finally delivered. With short cycles and such a frequent delivery of releases, the customer's trust in receiving the promised functionalities is built much more rapidly.

Planning

Management typically assumes that project members will need a specific amount of time to plan an application and some more time to develop it, so that when the deadline arises, the team will (hopefully) be able to present a running system. An agile process intends to present a running system not only at the end of the project but as soon as the first release, after three months (at the latest), and then regularly, after every release cycle.

This requires a completely different kind of planning. For instance, you cannot expect a final plan at the beginning of a project. Instead, planning will be an ongoing task. Furthermore, a typical plan based on components will not help you any further. The main difference is that such a component-based plan mainly (if not *only*) considers dependencies and does not center on the existence of an application that is almost always able to run. The idea of agile processes is to deliver early and often. Of course, the deliverables must always attain the current highest business value for the customer. In each iteration, a complete base functionality should be developed, whereas at the end of a release, the complete domain functionality should be available for use by the customer.

Therefore, at the beginning of each development cycle, the customer is required to define the functionality that provides the highest business value. The evaluation of the functionalities could change over time. For example, according to a shift in the market, the customer might prefer one functionality over another. Also, it may be more important for the customer to see the main functionality running earlier, rather than the optional behavior. But the decision is always the customer's. When the plan relies instead on components, it does not typically make a difference if a functionality has a main part and several optional ones—the unit under plan is the complete component.

A classic component-based plan might imply that the requirements are assumed to be fixed at the beginning of the project. The plan is then defined according to these requirements. But, as we all know, requirements tend to change over time, so the plan is quickly rendered invalid. And, with changing requirements, changing dependencies most often follow. But remember, plans based on components usually rely mainly on those dependencies. The requirements typically change because the customer learns more about the system as time goes on, so his or her understanding of it grows. The goal of delivering a running system early and often is intended, among other benefits, to help the customer gain a better understanding of the system.

On a large project, changing to agile planning requires convincing the project planning and controlling department (which I discuss in Chapter 6) to abandon the component-based plan.

Result-Oriented Planning

The plan for an agile project starts with development of the most important area of functionality, to provide the highest business value for the customer and to support the customer in shaping the system.

There are several nice side effects of presenting results early and always having a working system available:

- Seeing a running system motivates the project members more than just developing against a plan.
- Working software has always been a good marketing instrument that can be used inside and outside the company.

- There is no better way to test the load capacity and performance of the underlying architecture.
- Acceptance tests can be carried out early on.
- Users can provide feedback based on their real experience with the system.
- Learning to finish something regularly helps to establish a culture of achievement.
- If the system cannot be finished before the deadline, at least there will be a running system available for the customer, with the most important functions working.

These are the main reasons that an agile process is always based on result-oriented planning. However, your goal is not only to develop a result, but also, more importantly, to enable the customer to actually look at and use the software. Depending on the technology, this could provide another challenge. The simplest presentation is through a link on the intranet (maybe on the wiki), connecting to the latest release. If for some reason this is not possible, then you will probably have to manually install the software at the client's site. The value of frequent feedback will probably outweigh the cost of installing the system, even if it has to be done manually. Furthermore, installing it manually several times will probably lead to the requirement of automating this process.

Setting very short development cycles sometimes makes it difficult to deliver *complete* domain functionality at the end of a cycle, because developing the functionality may require more time than a cycle allows. In such a case, you have several options:

- An obvious option is to increase the time allocated to the cycle, sacrificing the benefit of shorter cycles. Unfortunately, you will only be able to correct the development direction after you find out what the actual software is doing, which you can only do when the application is actually running. It is much more difficult for the customer to get a better understanding without seeing the system.
- Your other option is to consider leaving the cycle's functionality incomplete. This is a well-known approach in industry and is known as following a component-based plan. Unfortunately, you will never know if the functionality you are developing is attaining the highest business

value for the customer, and you will still have to find out if the software is really working. As long as the functionality is not complete, there is no (easy) way to run any acceptance test against the output.

None is satisfying, so consider these:

- Insist on breaking functionality down so that only the most basic elements are included. Often, people tend to develop the whole functionality at once, without realizing that the business process hides, for example, a normal case, some exceptional cases, and some alternative cases. The customer will probably decide that the normal case is the most important one because it provides the highest business value and might require only one development cycle.
- If there is really no way of splitting up the task without omitting functionality, you will have to make an exception and allow the team to plan the iteration over more than one release cycle. In my experience (which is based on release cycles with a maximum of four weeks), there is never any need to spread this over more than two release cycles. If the developers ask for this, you can be sure that they did not try hard enough to break down the functionality.

The first of the last two options is preferable. Using the second solution always has the risk that people will make a habit of asking to spread functionality over three or four cycles, which contradicts the whole idea of short development cycles. The team will especially miss the motivation it could otherwise get from finishing a task at the end of a release cycle. But often the team hardly recognizes that this is the price for lazy planning. Laziness is another reason why people sometimes tend to ask for longer cycles.

Breaking up functionality is very difficult and requires a lot of discipline. But if you want to design and implement the functionality, you have to do this anyway—and of course, you have to understand, at least roughly, what this functionality is all about. So, agile methods ask us to shift the task of breaking up the functionality, which normally happens during design and development, to release and iteration planning.

In general, the plan gets more accurate the closer you are to the time you are planning. Thus, subteams will develop the detailed plan right before the next iteration. The project plan should not rely on components, as would be typical on large projects, but instead on the functionalities covered by the different release cycles. And, finally, the selected functionality should be determined by the customer, to ensure that he or she selects the functionality providing the highest business value.

Planning Tools

Every subteam should develop a detailed plan right before the iteration. So-called conservative tools, like whiteboards and index cards, are often the best means for coordinating this activity. For reporting the results to the project planning and controlling department, a simple text editor or the wiki Web is usually sufficient.

Iteration planning using a flip chart ...

Typically, the planning and controlling department is already familiar with a particular planning tool. If this is the case, I suggest you stick with that tool, assuming your experiences with it are positive. I further recommend developing only a rough plan with the tool—so refrain from giving details and stick to general information instead.

However, if your team is distributed, tools like XpPlanIt or XPlanner can be very helpful in coordinating your planning effort.[1]

Integration

Integration is one of the most difficult tasks in development with large teams. It is only after a successful integration that the effort from all the different teams on the project becomes visible and testable. Integration requires a huge amount of coordination effort and is a technical challenge, but it can be made easier by using tools.

It is common sense that integration should be done centrally, otherwise it would not be integration but several subintegrations, which in turn would all have to be integrated later on, anyway. Consequently, integration is a bottleneck, and it is more difficult the more that must be integrated.

Teams often argue that they cannot establish short development cycles because integration takes so long (or they fear that it will take too long). They prefer to integrate as seldom as possible. Sometimes, they even defer integration to the very end of development. However, integration is always more difficult if you have to integrate a lot of changes. The more often you integrate, the better you get in terms of tools, coordination, and technology. So, you might have to invest in integration at the beginning in order to benefit from it later on.

Normal-sized (small) agile teams often integrate using a token or a single integration machine: Only the team member having the token or sitting at the integration machine is allowed to integrate local changes with the common code base. With large teams, neither the token nor the integration machine is in sight of everybody. Of course, you can consider passing the integration token via e-mail, but even then, you may find that integration (which includes

---

[1]For XpPlanIt, see http://xpplanit.canoo.com/; for XPlanner, see http://www.xplan ner.org/.

running all tests) takes so long that it will be completely impossible for several teams to integrate frequently.

Basically, for large teams, you have to come up with an integration strategy that enables you to deal with the challenge: The integration bottleneck takes a significant amount of time, yet integrating frequently is very important. Before I go into this strategy, I would like to introduce the two principal approaches of integration:

- **Individual integration:** With this approach, one integrates one change after the other. The main advantage of this is that it makes it easy to detect conflicts in development efforts. Integrating the changes one after another means that each developer's efforts can only conflict with the system, not with the development efforts of another developer.

  The extreme approach to individual integration is *continuous integration:* Whenever a development task is finalized, it is integrated with the system. The advantage of continuous integration is that the deltas of the system are much smaller, and therefore the risk of conflict is lower. Moreover, the more often you integrate, the more often you will see improvements to the system, which will motivate the team. But unfortunately, integrating the effort of a large team requires a lot of work, so much that the goal of continuous integration is often unreachable.

- **Cumulative integration:** Using this approach, one integrates multiple changes at once. This approach requires that all teams deliver their development effort at the same, specified time. This strategy eliminates the scheduling problem encountered with individual integration, but it will make error detection much more difficult since the pool of changes that may have caused the error will be so large.

  One widely known method of cumulative integration is the nightly build. For this kind of integration strategy, all the development effort of the day is delivered to a single release and integration point in the evening, and integration takes place overnight. This is a good idea if your integration management runs smoothly. If it requires human interaction, it might be more difficult. I have worked with some large teams that established nightly builds, but it took them each nearly two years to set up this mechanism so that it worked efficiently.

In principle, the first approach seems to be easier because it is straightforward to detect and correct conflicts and errors. However, this approach has its limitations with large teams. The main reason it is so difficult is that a large team produces a lot of code (in theory, anyway), which often takes a while to build and test. For instance, assume it takes three hours to integrate and the project consists of fifteen different teams. That means that forty-five hours are required for integration, where a typical labor week consists of only forty hours. This makes it impossible to deal with integration the way I would on a typical Extreme Programming project, where integration is likely to take five minutes or less.

Integration Strategy

So, what is your integration strategy? Your integration mechanism probably does not allow nightly builds yet, but you still want to be able to integrate as often as possible so you can always have a running system available. Therefore, you must decide what would constitute the largest time frame that would be acceptable between integrations. In short, this time frame is at maximum the same as the length of each iteration; otherwise, you won't be able to present an integrated (and running) system at the end of each iteration.

Generally, the more frequently you are able to integrate, the better off you are. It will take time to establish the integration mechanism at the beginning of the project, but this will help you spot possibilities for reducing integration time later on. Luckily, at the start of development, integration is not too difficult, because there are not a lot of dependencies in place (and thus not a lot of conflicts), and there is not too much code available. So, the start is a good time to practice integration without too much risk.

Integration Team

To establish a smooth integration strategy, consider assembling a separate team that's responsible for this task. However, this does not mean that the integration team would be the only team responsible for integration. Integration should always be the responsibility of all team members. Each team has to integrate its own development effort both internally and with the teams on which it depends. The integration team should only accept code that has been pre-integrated.

Therefore, with a large team, your best bet is to use a combined integration strategy: Use individual integration—or continuous, if possible—for internal subteam integration, and cumulative integration—nightly builds, if possible—for integrating the efforts of all subteams. This way, every developer integrates his or her completed efforts with the subteam's. Then, at a predetermined time, all the subteams cumulatively deliver their development efforts to the project's single release point for integration. This requires that several changes from different teams be integrated at once. Furthermore, every development team has to work closely with the integration team whenever a problem in their area pops up.

At any level, every integration concludes with the running of all technical (unit) tests and a smoke test. According to author Steve McConnell, the aim of a smoke test is to

> . . . exercise the entire system from end to end. It does not have to be exhaustive, but it should be capable of exposing major problems. The smoke test should be thorough enough that if the build passes, you can assume that it is stable enough to be tested more thoroughly.[2]

In other words, the smoke test ensures that the application is doing something and does not crash immediately after start-up. If the application passes the smoke test, further acceptance tests (which I discuss in Chapter 5) will ensure the quality of the system.

The integration team serves as the single release and integration point, which means it provides the only way to integrate the whole system. Because of the important service this team provides, it obviously plays a key role on the project. It collects all changes, maintains the progress of the project, and in doing so measures the project status.

---

[2]Steve McConnell, "Best Practices: Daily Build and Smoke Test," *IEEE Software*, Vol. 13, No. 4 (July 1996), p. 144.

This key role has to be respected with good support and appropriate resources. My rule of thumb is that the project team will need 10 percent of the project members; so, with a hundred project members, you will have an integration team of ten. At the same time, the integration team should be treated as a regular team. This may seem like a contradiction until you consider these two points:

- The distinguishing characteristic of this team is that if it does not perform, the whole project comes to a halt, whereas if the same happens to another subteam, it will just stop the development in its area. This is why the integration team must be given extra support—any problem it encounters must be assigned the highest priority. After all, if the integration team is unable to integrate, it must have quick access to the corresponding developer, who must either resolve the problem or withdraw the code from integration.
- The integration team is a regular subteam, though, in the sense that it should plan, test, and implement its tasks like all the other teams. These tasks typically relate to improving the integration mechanism by creating corresponding scripts, so like other teams, the integration team also benefits from reviews and refactoring. Without reviews and refactoring, the risk is high that the team will not provide sufficient support, which in turn will result in slow integration and endless build and configuration cycles.

Tools for Configuration Management and Version Control

Using an incremental and iterative approach requires the use of tools for configuration management and version control. Both enable developers to go back to earlier versions. Using version control, you can go back to an earlier version of, for example, a method or a class. It also enables you to compare different versions and confirm you are using the correct one. Using configuration management, you can go back to another version or configuration of the whole system. Thus, these tools allow you to define a baseline, for the whole system, that you can deliver as a release to your customer. Even as development proceeds after a release, the configuration management tool will allow you to go back to the delivered version. There are some free tools in this area, such as cvs.[3] If you are performing continuous integration, tools such as CruiseControl or IntegrationGuard are especially supportive and freely available.[4]

Nowadays, it is becoming more and more common to use an integrated development environment for implementing software. An integrated development environment consists of (at the very least) an editor, compiler, and debugger. Most often, you will find that these tools have a great connection to some common version and configuration management systems, and sometimes they also offer a graphical user interface builder. Most of the currently available tools also have the corresponding unit test tool integrated, although most of them belong to the Java family. For example, an integrated development environment for Java has JUnit, a unit test tool for Java, integrated. If the programming language allows it, it is advantageous to change the code and variables in the debugger and execute it therein. As mentioned earlier, Eclipse is an integrated development environment that supports several programming languages and is freely available.[5]

Retrospectives

An agile development process distinguishes itself from a linear one by being flexible and changeable. Thus, the agile process requires you to regard critically not only the project's progress, but also the current support of the process. This critical process inspection results in continuous changes to the process—to better support the actual circumstances. It is not a good idea to define a process without consulting the project members; a process will only work if the project members accept it. Of course, it always helps if you can

---

[3]For cvs, see http://www.cvshome.org/.

[4]ForCruiseControl, see http://cruisecontrol.sourceforge.net; for IntegrationGuard, see http://iguard.sourceforge.net.

[5]For Eclipse, see http://www.eclipse.org/.

help the project members identify with the process, or if you find a simple way to shape the process to support them best.

It will be very difficult to define the process completely at the beginning of the project. No process is ideal for all purposes (for all project sizes, organizational cultures, technologies, people, and the like). Similarly, no fixed process serves the project optimally at the *beginning* of the project as well as at the *end*, since so many things will change over time—for example, the team's habits may improve or the teams may jell better. Thus, the process will only be finalized at the end of the project.

Only through continuous adaptation of the process during project development is the process able to support project members at an optimum level. Appropriately enough, the main characteristic of all agile processes is the possibility of adapting the process.

Retrospectives are the most important means of helping your team adapt the process. A retrospective inspects the project state, uncovers problems, but also questions the current process.[6] Retrospectives on the status of the project typically take place after each iteration, and the ones with a special focus on process improvement take place after each release.

Thus, a retrospective covers two levels: The first level reflects on the evolution of the software. The second level, often called the *meta* level, inspects the actual process. Both have a major impact on the success of a project.

Attendance

Although developers are the ones who will mainly shape the process, the size of the team often prohibits having *all* project members participate in the retrospective. Therefore, I suggest you ask the teams to each designate one representative to attend the retrospectives. You could also ask for floating attendance, so that for each retrospective, each team chooses a different representative. These representatives are asked to inform their teams of what happens during the retrospectives. You can ensure that those unable to attend can find out what happened in the retrospective by providing this information via the intranet. A wiki Web would be a good

---

[6]For more on retrospectives, see Norman L. Kerth, *Project Retrospectives: A Handbook for Team Reviews* (New York: Dorset House Publishing, 2001).

place, if you have one installed, because it will further allow those who didn't attend to comment on the information.

For some results of the developers' retrospective, it might not be enough to simply inform the rest of the project team; the team may have to follow up on the outcomes and take action. If this is the case, you have to ensure that the teams take these actions.

Although the developers are mainly responsible for shaping the process, management occasionally has some requirements for the process. Therefore, you should invite management to the retrospectives. However, pick the management representatives carefully, to ensure a safe environment. You may want to delay this invitation for a few retrospectives, until the team feels safe enough to articulate all issues openly, in front of a management representative. The teams may initiate the invitation if they find that a change in the process requires the approval of management (for example, regarding budget or political acceptance).

In one of my projects, management was quite eager to participate in the retrospective. The teams were not very excited about the idea and refused to accept it, at first. There was a misconception that people would be punished for voicing their opinions and problems, yet I had neither encountered nor heard of such a thing happening in that company. It took me a while to convince them that this was actually a great opportunity for them to formulate their issues in front of the people who have the power to make the appropriate changes.

Retrospectives can be a big hit among team members. They are often the only forum where the teams get to exchange their experiences. They also provide a great environment for integrating external teams (discussed further in Chapter 6). Therefore, do not be surprised if retrospectives become very popular, with a lot of people asking to attend.

Techniques

Retrospectives can be one of the most important steps in agile development because they help shape the process. Therefore, you will need to obtain open and honest comments from all team members in order to know what kind of refinements to the process are necessary. Although this is the main purpose of the retrospective, it might be a good idea to offer a forum for team members to provide these comments during development time, so that no important issues are forgotten before the retrospective. A wiki Web or personal interviews by the communication team (mentioned in Chapter 3) may serve well for this purpose.

You can lead retrospectives by using an open discussion format. This format will be adequate if there already is a safe environment for open discussion, or if the reflection focuses mainly on the status of the project and not on shaping the process, although the former undoubtedly influences the latter. A safe environment is one in which participants are not scared to articulate their issues and will thus communicate their concerns in an open and honest manner. Their fear often results from social constraints in the group. To address those fears, the moderator should have the following qualifications:

- **Listening:** You have to be comfortable with silence. Some people need time for creative thinking. You would destroy this by breaking the silence.
- **Discretion:** The participants should share their experiences. It is not your role to teach them what you have learned; they should learn from one another.
- **Questions:** By using open questions, you encourage the participants to further share their experiences, signaling to them that this is important information.
- **Honor contributions:** Again, listen to, and do not judge, what people say. Make sure that the other participants follow your lead by accepting each contribution.
- **Summarize:** So that no one loses focus, summarize the important points. Represent these points visually and ensure that everybody knows which topic to work on.

Especially on the metalevel, you will achieve much greater success if you use creative moderation formats, instead of open discussions. These moderation techniques can help you create a safe environment. As a starting point for performing retrospectives, you can use for example the metaplan technique or Open Space Technology, which are both described below, in more detail. They both are easy to implement and are quite efficient. I have used both techniques regularly in retrospectives—all of which were scheduled for ninety minutes. Both techniques scale rather well. I have used them for groups of ten to a hundred people, but I find them more difficult to employ with the smaller groups. A group of twenty to fifty people is perhaps ideal.

METAPLAN TECHNIQUE

This technique is fairly well known, and it works very well because most of the articulation is done anonymously. However, it more or less lacks the power of creative group thinking and discussing.

Anonymous feedback …

You will need a lot of index cards of two different colors. In the first iteration, participants should articulate "all things that worked well" on one color and "all things that have to be improved" on the different colored cards. The two colors make the cards easier to sort. Insist on having only one issue per card. The "issue" can be almost anything—it can be related to the process itself, to development, to the organization, to management, and so on.

Collect the cards and separate them by color. Stick them on metaplan stands. It is likely that you will have more "requires improvement" cards than "doing fine" cards at the beginning of the project. You will realize after a few retrospectives that fewer cards get filled out as the process becomes more accepted and shaped according to the team's needs.

Ask all participants to come up with useful categories into which the cards fit and ask them to sort the cards according to these categories. Use this step to eliminate duplicated cards and to keep a record of how often each topic is mentioned—this communicates the importance of the topic.

In the next step, participants form groups based on their interest in categories. Invite each group to work on how to improve the things that don't work well or to emphasize the things that do.

To round up this session, you will have to assign people responsibility for the different tasks. More precisely, you will ask the participants to take responsibility for particular tasks. Finally, the participants prioritize and estimate the tasks. It is a good idea to come up with the three most pressing tasks, those that the team would like to focus on during the next development cycle.

MODIFIED OPEN SPACE TECHNOLOGY

This technique is related to Open Space Technology, but also has roots in the pattern-mining area. It is not as anonymous as the metaplan technique, so if the group does not feel safe, it might not work. On the other hand, it enables creative thinking.

People like to complain about things much more than they like to praise things. This trait can be used effectively with this technique.

Make sure to provide enough flip charts, and that the flip charts can be stuck to the wall. Participants are first asked to focus on problems. You can use the same question as above—what needs to be improved? Ask the attendees to write each problem on a separate flip chart. To emphasize problems, you might want to write them in red. As soon as a problem is written on the paper, publish it by taping it to the wall. This is a parallel task—everybody writes problems and publishes them at the same time. Once this is done, the exhibition is officially open. The participants then walk around and either publish more problems or write their comments on already published ones.

Next, the task is to come up with solutions to problems. The attendees will still walk around the exhibition, but they are now asked to think about appropriate solutions to the problems. They might still write down their comments, which can relate either to the problems or to the solution. The comment could be something like, *"I think this solution cannot work, because . . ."* or *"I have seen this solution working already—project X used to do it this way. . . ."* These comments often suggest factors that have to be considered when seeking a solution. Some of these comments might just point to helpful sources of further information, such as people whose experience might prove valuable.

This will lead directly to the next step: Participants should write their name on the flip charts, to take responsibility for working on a problem, or they should write the name of an expert who might be interested in bearing the responsibility. At the end, there should be at least one person responsible for resolving each problem. If there isn't, you have to conclude that the problem is not really of interest and thus not important.

All these steps usually run in parallel, which means that although the focus might, at the moment, be on solutions, forgotten problems are still allowed to be published. Furthermore, the discussion of problems and solutions is always welcome.

The end of this session is more traditional: Ask the participants to prioritize the problems, to estimate the needed resources for the solution (time, money, and so on), and to come up with at least the top three problems they would like to focus on during the next development cycle. If the environment is not safe yet, ask them to make the prioritization anonymously.

Learning to Become Great
by Joshua Kerievsky and Diana Larsen

> The team that became great didn't start off great—it learned how to produce extraordinary results.
>
> —Peter Senge[7]

Most of the large Extreme Programming (XP) groups we've coached didn't start off great. They became great over successive iterations by learning how to improve. While XP's practices help individuals, pairs, and teams learn to improve, the two practices that stand out the most in their ability to help teams and whole organizations produce extraordinary results are project chartering and project retrospectives.[8]

Project chartering helps project communities answer questions like

- Is the idea for the project worthwhile?
- How does the project further the organization's vision/mission?
- How will we know if the project is a success?
- Who is part of the project community?

Like refactoring, project chartering is an ongoing endeavor. Writing and revising a charter requires a rigorous inquiry into the project's

- vision and mission
- project community
- values (what are the community's five most important values?)

---

[7]Peter Senge, *The Fifth Discipline: The Art & Practice of the Learning Organization* (New York: Currency Doubleday, 1990), p. 4.

[8]Project chartering happens when the project team and management develop a shared understanding (a jointly defined charter) that defines what has to be done, how it has to be done, when it will be done, who will do it, and what objectives will be reached with it.

- committed resources
- management tests (measure of internal and external success)
- boundaries and limits
- working agreements

Project chartering does not take the place of release and iteration planning; rather, it provides direction for those adaptive planning activities. Project communities that learn to practice successful project chartering often obtain professional help with this practice, since this kind of highly collaborative and adaptive chartering differs greatly from traditional project chartering.

Management tests are a key part of project chartering. These tests complement XP projects' unit tests and storytests by adding a test layer around the project itself.[9] While unit tests assert that small units of code meet programmer expectations, and storytests assert that system features meet customer expectations, management tests assert that organizational returns on investment meet management expectations.

Project retrospectives are another highly effective group and organizational learning tool.[10] By taking the time to look back over the course of a project, a project community can discover how it can improve for future projects. The investment of two or three days in a project retrospective often produces an excellent return on investment. Such end-of-project retrospectives are especially useful when project communities are large, since the size of a group can make it difficult for members to learn about all significant occurrences throughout a project. For example, five months after a retrospective Diana facilitated with 74 members of a project community, one project manager said,

---

[9]"Storytest" is another term for "acceptance test."

[10]Project retrospectives always take place at the end of a project, whereas "normal" retrospectives take place during the project.

After the project retrospective, there was a strong feeling that there needed to be follow-throughs on the plan we developed for changes in the way that releases were organized, and we have implemented new project teams as a result. We have also pushed accountability and responsibility for the content of the releases down to individual project teams and managers, which was something that people asked for during the retrospective. We are now holding more cross-functional meetings and transfer of information meetings to improve people's understanding of what is being worked on and to find out if there are any concerns or issues that need to be resolved for the release. We are also forming teams to define process improvements based on best practices across all projects. I think that a lot of good information has been transferred to the people working on the next series of releases. It's hoped that they will be able to build on the successes identified in the project retrospective and that these releases will be the basis for even more successes and improvements.

Many of the improvements this manager mentioned were things that people had been talking about among themselves for months, but those discussions by themselves never developed the momentum necessary to actually make the desired changes happen. The critical mass and common understanding to effect real change came as a result of a project retrospective. And the results of this work fed directly into the planning, risk-management, and project chartering for the next project. The team referenced in the above quote has not yet made the shift to agile software development, but as you can tell from the manager's remarks, they are getting closer all the time.

In summary, we have found that for most large XP groups to become great, a culture of learning and improvement must flourish. Project chartering and project retrospectives help make that happen.

Getting Started with an Agile Process

Each project has different starting conditions. When establishing an agile process, you should be aware of those conditions and set up the process accordingly. Thus, how to start depends mainly on the status of the project. To figure out what this is, it is helpful to ask the following questions:

- Is the project just about to start from scratch?
- Does the project have a previous history? For instance, has it been canceled before, so that all its hopes for success now rely on the new start using an agile process?
- Is the project under way, but not running as smoothly as you would like, with no outcome in sight?
- Was the project under way, with everything going fine, when somebody had the idea that installing an agile process would be cool or might improve things?

The different answers to these questions influence not only the way the agile process will be set up, but also the issues you will have to deal with. For example, if the project has failed before and is now starting all over again, you will most likely find all members of the team very frustrated about having their last few months of hard work thrown in the trash. Also, the people responsible for the failed project will probably not believe in the success of the restart. Thus, in this environment, you will find a lot of mistrust and frustration paired with a desire to do everything differently than before. If the project is already successfully under way but somebody wants to switch the process because he or she read in a magazine that agile processes are cool, you will find a lot of (justified) resistance to the change.

Make sure you understand the situation before you start unintentionally overwhelming the team.

Learn from History

Whatever the reason is for switching to an agile process, you will always have to deal with people who have some experience in software development. One very rare exception is when the whole team has been assembled from recent college graduates. Because this situation is so rare, though, I won't cover this challenge here.

Normally, the history or experience of each project member is a great and important source to learn from. Therefore, make use of this available experience. Depending on the size of the team, it will probably not be possible to talk to each and every member individually. So you might have to consider using some of the group moderation techniques mentioned above. However, at the beginning of a new or restarted project, the risk is high that people will not feel safe enough for a group session. This is why it is often better to randomly pick people and interview them. It will definitely be much easier for them to talk openly and honestly about their experiences in a one-on-one setting.

Learn from history ...

To get a rather complete picture, it is helpful to select a representative amount of people as interview partners. Furthermore, it is important to interview some people who know the company quite well, because they can point out the typical traps in the organization. Make sure that you cover the following questions in the interviews:

- What did you like in the projects you have worked on so far?
- What could have been improved?

- What problems have always been pointed out but ignored?
- What would you rate as the highest risks for projects in this company?
- Do you know of an existing enterprise-wide process and, if so, is it used successfully?
- If this project has a previous history, why do you believe

  - the project was canceled?
  - it runs so smoothly?
  - it runs so badly?

The answers to these questions provide a good starting point for the process you want to begin with. You will have a feel for things that have to be emphasized, improved, and avoided. Often, you will get important information about typical traps. This information sensitizes your awareness, which will enable you to react to these traps as soon as they pop up. Moreover, you will find out what kind of support people expect from a development process.

Start Small

Make sure that the initial starting team consists of fewer than twenty people, preferably between six and twelve. If you already have one hundred project people sitting around (if, for example, the project is a restart), prepare them with training in the technology and ask them to familiarize themselves with the domain.

If you start with a larger team, the system will be defined by the size of the team.[11] For instance, if you start with ten subteams, the system will always be partitioned into ten parts, although this kind of separation may be neither requested nor appropriate for the system. This leads to a fragile architecture and to poor design decisions.

The initial team has the task of developing from the business domain the functionality that will provide a first business value. This first business functionality is called a *referential implementation* of the architecture. We call it referential implementation because it serves as an example on which to expand the system and as a basis to learn more about the business domain and the technology. In

---

[11]Thanks to Mike Cohn for pointing this out.

order for this referential implementation to evolve, the initial team also has to enable this development by implementing the base for this functionality, often called the core architecture. This is important: The team should not start designing an architecture from scratch; it should come up with a referential implementation that will contain an underlying architecture as well as some real functionality out of the business domain. Therefore, the architecture will evolve (and not be created) from the very beginning and will define the technical frame for the business domain.

The starting team should consist of people with different skills and backgrounds. You will probably need the majority to have good technical backgrounds, but you will also need some business domain experts—without them, you will not be able to prove that the architecture works in the business domain and, as such, the referential implementation cannot serve as a reference point for the releases that follow.

You should allow the starting team to reflect on its efforts after completion. The team definitely will have learned numerous lessons that are worth thinking about. This reflection will produce essential knowledge about the system and will also give the team some ideas on how to grow. The reflection, which could be set up like a retrospective, should focus mainly on the things that need to be improved and on the things that need to be kept. Moreover, the reflection should also ensure that everybody from the starting team has a good understanding of the implementation. Later on, this team will serve as the knowledge center as the team is expanded. If time permits, allow people on the starting team to improve the referential implementation according to their findings in the reflection. Make sure, however, that they do not try to develop a "perfect" architecture without involving domain teams that are responsible for specifying the architecture requirements.

Finalizing the Architecture

After the referential implementation is complete, the starting team often has a lot of ideas about what should be improved, and how to develop not only a really good solution but also the *world's best* architecture. You have to balance the following arguments and decide how good will be good enough for your architecture:

- Everybody would be proud to call his or her own architecture the best that has ever been developed, but the domain teams won't profit from unnecessary flexibility.
- If the rest of the team has already been assembled, all the other project members are probably waiting to start their work. They probably won't be able to contribute a lot to the discussion because they do not know much about the architecture built so far, and thus they don't know if they need a better one. They will, though, probably be afraid to start developing if the architecture is not stable (or finalized).
- The customer is more interested in functionality than in how great the architecture is, mainly because he or she will neither see the architecture nor *directly* benefit from it.

Although all these arguments should be respected, the customer's lines of reasoning carry the most weight. This does not mean that you should never build anything in your system that is not directly visible to the customer; however, you should only build what is needed in the development of some functionality.

Allowing the architecture to improve can also provide a psychological problem. As mentioned above, developers tend to resist using something that is not yet finalized. They fear that all their effort will be thrown out if the architecture changes. But, on the other hand, the team cannot judge, yet, how much it might benefit from shaping the architecture itself. So far, I have never found a way to assure the teams in advance that the benefits of a changeable architecture are much greater than the cost of any lost effort. A strategy that works for me is to *declare* the architecture stable and finalized. This takes away the fear of the developers, allowing them to start developing. Typically, it does not take too long before they start asking for small (and later on, for bigger) changes in the architecture so it can better serve their needs. This trick of declaring the architecture stable is one used by a lot of other change agents in agile development.

Grow Slowly

In any case, you will need knowledge transfer, further functionality development, *plus* a simple, flexible architecture. You will definitely encounter fewer problems if you allow the team to grow slowly. As stated earlier, you should use the starting team as the core for the knowledge transfer. Its members will have to serve as coaches for the new people on the team. The slower the team grows, the more likely it is to jell, and the better the knowledge will be spread. This is because the slower you expand the team, the easier it is to use the best medium for knowledge transfer—direct communication.

If the whole team is already assembled, then there probably is not enough time to grow slowly. It is likely that the financial controller is telling you every day how much money the project loses with all the people sitting around, not being productive. If this is the case, then you have to balance your knowledge with management's wishes very carefully: If you integrate everyone on the team at once, you may lose even more money in the long-term because knowledge transfer will be so difficult. You do not want to overburden the starting team with this task. On the other hand, you might have a starting team that is able to integrate and coach one hundred people.

You probably do not want to manage hundreds of people working on the project as a single team. Instead, you want to establish several subteams (discussed in Chapter 3), which will make up the whole project team. This is much easier than managing one huge team, which provides a lot of management challenges. Furthermore, building the subteams empowers these teams to organize themselves (remember, the use of self-organizing teams is an underlying principle of the Agile Manifesto). The size and number of the subteams will define the number of coaches needed. You will profit the most if the coaches do not have to coach more than four or five people; in this case, each subteam might require more than one coach.

The difficulty in assigning coaches is that you might need some members of the starting team to improve the architecture according to the needs of the new teams. So, it would not be wise to ask everybody from the starting team to act as a coach. The only way that would be possible is if the whole team grows slowly.

Culture of Change

Changing means giving up a habit only to replace it with another habit. According to Virginia Satir, a change happens whenever a *foreign element* (any external stimuli) brings our status quo out of balance. The foreign element moves us into a status called *chaos*, also known as uncertainty. This uncertainty arises when the old status quo is not valid anymore, we have not found a new status quo yet, and we are still looking for one. This search can take a while, and once we have a *transforming idea* (an idea that helps us to understand the required change), we will be able to leave the chaos state and settle into our new (improved) status quo.[12]

Learning and Change Processes

The decision by a company to run some of its projects using an agile process implies that the company will undergo a major change. Any change involves a departure from the existing status quo, which is exchanged for a new, and hopefully better, status quo. This process is similar to the way we learn, as stated by Richard Beckhard and Wendy Pritchard in *Changing the Essence:*

> Learning and change processes are part of each other. Change is a learning process and learning is a change process.[13]

Therefore, in order to successfully install an agile process, a company has to be willing not only to change, but also to learn. Both of which imply letting go of a familiar and probably convenient environment, and swapping it with something unknown, which is always frightening.

---

[12]Virginia Satir, John Banmen, Jane Gerber, and Maria Gomori, *The Satir Model: Family Therapy and Beyond* (Palo Alto, Calif.: Science and Behavior Books, 1991).

[13]Richard Beckhard and Wendy Pritchard, *Changing the Essence: The Art of Creating and Leading Fundamental Change in Organizations* (New York: John Wiley & Sons, 1992), p. 14.

Neither learning nor change can be imposed on the organization. The people within the organization have to recognize the necessary changes on their own in order to give up their habits. To facilitate this, the organization must provide an environment that enables learning and change. In order to establish such a learning organization, the organization, or rather the staff, will have to reflect on its status quo and on its desired status. It is only in such an environment that team members will be able to discover what steps are required to reach the desired status. Introducing an agile process is a good start toward becoming a learning organization, because it is a major change.

Every agile process contains the following subtle steps:

- reflection
- learning
- change

Reflection is not only a self-reflection, it is, more importantly, a reflection on the feedback obtained.

Now that we have talked generally about change and learning, what does this mean in terms of agile development? We all know that requirements can and will change over time. But we still try in vain to prevent this from happening by using development processes that are unable to deal with these changing requirements. Jim Highsmith puts it best in his book *Adaptive Software Development*:

> Most management strategies are geared either to reduce the number of changes or to control changes. While these strategies are useful, it is more useful to embrace change than try to control it.[14]

Although it is common sense that the requirements will change, we still stick to the status quo of the established development process. What we need to do instead is to reflect on the situation; this will help us realize that requirements are in fact changing. In turn, we will learn that our process does not have a means to deal with

---

[14]James A. Highsmith III, *Adaptive Software Development: A Collaborative Approach to Managing Complex Systems* (New York: Dorset House Publishing, 2000), p. 183.

these changes and that we must look for another approach in order to deal with the situation. However, more often than not, we reflect and maybe we learn as well, but we still resist change.

It seems that we only embrace change when the *pressure of suffering* is so high that it is impossible to ignore the unsatisfactory nature of the status quo. In other words, we can only expect people, and therefore the organization, to change quickly once their current situation becomes unacceptable. Using the prevalent logic, the situation will be ignored if it can be: You could point out to team members the poor nature of the status quo, but because they don't want to face the difficulties that making the necessary change would bring, they might not experience the situation as being particularly miserable. So, whatever change you want to make that time will be difficult to impose. However, as soon as the team realizes how bad the situation is, you will be astonished at how quickly a change can be made. Therefore, the only way to make a cultural change is to sensitize people to the actual misery, so they feel the bad situation themselves. In such a situation, it is your task as the change agent to point out to team members how miserable the status quo is and make them aware that it is possible to reach a better state. But you need to be patient.

Introducing Change

As we discussed earlier in this chapter, not every change benefits from a smooth introduction. Sometimes, it is better to change something so radically that the change you originally wanted to make comes naturally with the exaggerated change.

Especially for a large project, continuous feedback is essential. For example, cycles for iterations and releases have to be much shorter than with smaller teams. In my experience, it's most important to obtain quick feedback on all kinds of things: the organization, the environment, running software, staff satisfaction, and the like. Quick feedback should be the first thing you introduce. There is no way you can smoothly introduce shorter feedback cycles. As soon as they are established, though, all other changes will follow more naturally.

When introducing a massive change like the switch to agile development, do not force all the changes at once. Some might not be acceptable for the whole team. If you force such a change, team members may try to undermine every future change you try to make. Remember, it might just be the wrong time for the introduction of this change. Therefore, it is sometimes better to just wait until a situation arises that makes this change a necessity for the whole team and not just the change agent. In that case, it will be much better accepted.

Although you have the best arguments for the change and you believe Confucius was right when he said, 2,500 years ago, that "Thinking is the noblest way of learning," your team may want to follow the "hardest way of learning: experience." You still have to respect that people hate change in general because they will always feel more comfortable in their existing situation than in an unfamiliar one (and they will typically believe that things can only get worse). People will only embrace change if their level of suffering overtakes their pain threshold. They have to admit to themselves that the only way out is to give up their old habits and go for the change.

Whenever there is resistance to a (necessary) change, suggest trying it at least for one development cycle. Sometimes, once they actually undertake the change, people are pleasantly surprised to find out that it is not as bad as they had assumed, and that it actually worked out very well. Thus, the pain they feared they would experience is often far greater than the actual pain. A lot of people experience this regularly when going to the dentist.[15] They often try to postpone medical treatment as long as possible because they are scared it will hurt. However, the pain suffered at the hands of the dentist is often not as bad as imagined. In the end, the benefit from the treatment is such a relief that afterward it is difficult for people to understand why they didn't go to the dentist sooner.

It is important that you remind the people regularly of the change. When undergoing a change, it is easy to fall back into your old habits. For example, say you know a little bit of Italian and more than a little bit of Spanish. If you then travel to Italy, you will often catch yourself using Spanish words instead of Italian words. The reason for this is that things that are more familiar to us are easier to use. Using and doing unfamiliar things always takes great effort.

---

[15]Thanks to Dierk König for sharing this metaphor.

121

Especially in a large team, you have to be aware that for some people, it will be easy to change whereas others will need more time and support.

Force Courage

Accepting and embracing change also means understanding that errors are part of the process. An agile process is not intended to "do it right the first time." Instead, it is based on the idea that this sends the wrong message. According to Jim Highsmith, expecting to get it right the first time implies that

- We can't be uncertain.
- We can't experiment.
- We can't learn from mistakes.
- We can't deviate from the plan.[16]

In summary, this strategy will prevent us from learning from experience. Naturally, we will get better over time, and it would be a waste of money not to profit from our learnings. Jim Highsmith summarized this message, not only for agile processes:

> Do not worry about getting it right the first time—worry about getting it right the last time.[17]

With the option of correcting a decision after we have made it (doing it right the last time), we have the ability to question the suitability of people to their roles. Many projects have failed due to people being in the wrong position.

For example, I have seen many good developers get offered management positions. However, not every good developer is a good leader.[18] If the developer accepts the position, you have two potential problems: You have lost a good developer, and you may have gained a poor leader. Often, people are unhappy if they occupy the wrong position, but it is still not easy for them to admit

---

[16]Highsmith, op. cit., p. 75.

[17]James A. Highsmith III, "Adaptive Software Development" (OOPSLA 2000, Minneapolis, 2000).

[18]It's common knowledge that everybody gets promoted until he or she reaches a position that's unsuitable.

that they would prefer to step down. Monetary reasons and reputation hinder them from following their conscience. Most of the time, your gut feeling will remind you of this bad situation, but there are also some more obvious indications: for example, if the newly bred manager is still doing part-time development or making technical decisions, not management decisions.[19]

To change such a situation, courage is required from both sides—the ones who suggested the change in position have to confess that this decision was wrong, and the person who is in the position has to admit that the role does not fit. But for the sake of the project's progress and for the satisfaction of the people, do not be afraid to point out necessary changes like this one.

Indicating such unsatisfying situations requires not only courage but honesty. Remember, it is always better to be honest—which helps build trust in the project—than to cover up some poor conditions. It is easiest, obviously, to be honest if you have good news. But in a sense, bad news *is* good news, because only if the unacceptable circumstances are known can people act and thus change things for the better.

Summary

Very large teams require very short cycles. The problem is: If this tanker we call software development cruises in the wrong direction, it is almost impossible to change course after a while. The course of the tanker needs to be constantly monitored, which is only possible by obtaining quick feedback. The feedback will always have an impact on the plan. Therefore, an agile approach is planning-driven instead of plan-driven. Or, as Dwight D. Eisenhower once stated,

A plan is nothing; planning is everything.

Integration is one of the most challenging topics, organizationally and technically, when developing with a large team. By balancing the effort it takes to set up a perfect integration environment and the benefit you will get out of it, you should always work on mak-

---

[19]Thanks to Dierk König for pointing this out.

ing integration smooth. Only this will allow you to get quick feedback on a running system.

An agile process will always change over time to give the best possible support for the project development. This means that whenever an agile process is explained in detail, it is only a snapshot of the process. The agility of the process allows you to constantly adapt the process to new circumstances. Thus, the essence of agile processes is that you look at how the system behaves under real-life circumstances and adjust it accordingly. These adjustments are mainly based on the results of retrospectives, so the project members are the ones shaping the process.

5

AGILITY AND TECHNOLOGY

An independent architect
shouldn't be guided by sensations,
but by reflections.
          —Hans Scharoun

M.E. Conway formulated a law in 1968, in an article he wrote for *Datamation*. The law is now widely known as Conway's Law:

> Organizations which design systems are constrained to produce systems which are copies of the communication structures of these organizations.[1]

This law has been taken even further by several unknown authors:[2]

- The architecture of a system is a copy of the architecture of the organization.
- The structure of a system is determined by the structure of the team.

---

[1]Melvin E. Conway, "How Do Committees Invent?" *Datamation*, Vol. 14, No. 4 (April 1968), p. 28.

[2]These statements can be found at http://c2.com/cgi/wiki?ConwaysLaw.

- To understand the team, look at the software it is producing. If it is slow and bloated, the team is slow and bloated. If it is lean and quick, the team is lean and quick.

All these experiences express different nontechnical influences on architecture. However, there is still one more major influence, best expressed by my colleague Nicolai Josuttis in the context of his experience as chief architect of a large mission-critical project:

> The size of a project, or rather of a team, influences the architecture.[3]

This chapter explores different perspectives on the architecture and describes the influence a large team has. We discuss the role of the architectural lead, the importance of a simple architecture, and the purpose of the architecture (or rather the team that produces it). Then, we discuss what circumstances can lead to notable bottlenecks, which can slow down the development progress tremendously. Next, we take a look at the impact of different ownership models and balance this with trust in the project members. At some point, you have to choose a technology for the development, so we talk about the impact of using cutting-edge technology. Finally, we talk about different techniques and good practices, which should help to facilitate implementing a system that allows change.

Architect and Architecture

The term "architecture" sounds very solid, which might contradict the intention of an agile process, and talking about an architectural lead in this context might further stress this impression. However, it is not important to be up-to-date. It is important to find the right means (established or otherwise) to create a flexible system that allows change even late in the project. Achieving this flexibility is mainly based on trust in the project members, combined with the important role of the architectural lead.

---

[3]Nicolai M. Josuttis, personal communication.

Architectural Lead

On a typical agile project with a small team, you will often end up
without an architectural lead because the whole team is of equal
value and takes the same responsibility for the whole project.
Although this could or should be a goal for a large team, too, it
would never work, because development would diverge, uncoordinated.

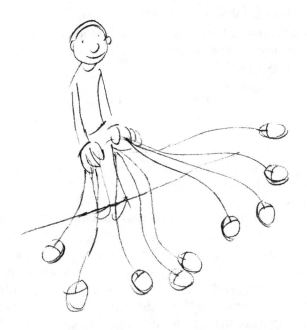

Somebody should pull the strings ...

As the old saying goes, too many cooks spoil the broth. With a
huge amount of people on a team, you would most likely end up
with a huge number of concepts and ideas in the system. These
different concepts and ideas are likely to contradict one another.
So, what you need instead is conceptual integrity, which is the
most important quality in a large system, as Fred Brooks states:

> It is better to have a system omit certain anomalous fea-
> tures and improvements, but to reflect one set of design

127

ideas, than to have one that contains many good but independent and uncoordinated ideas.[4]

An architectural lead can help you take a big step toward conceptual integrity. Next to architectural guidance, there are other important reasons for requesting an architectural lead. Often, you will find that not everybody on the team is able to describe the big picture necessary to make the right decisions. Without this big picture in mind, again according to Brooks,

> On large teams, subteams tend to suboptimize to meet their own targets, rather than think about the total effect on the user. This breakdown in orientation is a major hazard of large projects.[5]

The lead architect is the one who will always be able to describe the system and help everybody see the big picture, or as Alistair Cockburn writes,

> This person's contribution is to keep memories of key ideas alive on changing development teams.[6]

This is important for people inside and outside the project—the lead architect will serve as the main contact person for specific questions. Without this main contact person, a large team would soon drop into chaos. The principal reason is that all team members would be uncertain about the assignment of responsibility and about who would make the final decisions (as we discussed in Chapter 3). These are the responsibilities of the architectural lead. Consequently, he or she is the one who pulls the strings. The architectural lead should also train the team members by helping them, for example, to see the big picture and to take up responsibility. So, the lead architect will not only be the one memorizing the key ideas, but more importantly, the one who spreads these ideas so

---

[4]Frederick P. Brooks, Jr., *The Mythical Man-Month: Essays on Software Engineering*, 20th anniv. ed. (Reading, Mass.: Addison-Wesley, 1995), p. 42.
[5]Ibid. p. 238.
[6]Alistair Cockburn, *Agile Software Development* (Reading, Mass.: Addison-Wesley, 2002), p. 99.

that more and more people will have the same understanding of the system.

Simple Architecture

One of the key ideas an architectural lead of an agile project should have in mind is to work toward the goal of a simple architecture. According to David Parnas, this is the first step in the direction already defined by the main purpose of the architectural lead:

> Simplicity comes from conceptual integrity.[7]

Focusing on a simple architecture is consistent with the KISS approach, to Keep It Simple, Stupid. The architecture has to be simple in order to fully serve the needs of a large team:

- If the architecture is not complex, it will be understandable to *ordinary* project members. Therefore, simplicity should always be favored over complexity.
- The architecture will have to change over time, to meet changed requirements (or the needs of the domain teams). Therefore, the architecture should be flexible and easy to change.

From this, it should be obvious that the architecture has to respect the circumstances of the environment, namely the organization of the project.

The underlying architecture should also go through continuous refactoring, like the rest of the application. However, refactoring and changing the architecture does not necessarily mean continuously introducing new functionality. It means eliminating obsolete parts to further simplify the architecture. Along these lines, Paul B. MacCready, of AeroVironment, explained that the development of the award-winning human-powered aircraft, the Gossamer Condor, didn't stop once it was in the air. Instead, the aircraft was continuously made simpler and lighter:

---

[7]David Parnas, "XP—Extremely What?" (International Conference on eXtreme Programming and Agile Processes in Software-Engineering 2002, Sardinia, Italy, 2002).

If a part broke, we replaced it with a member that was heavier and sturdier. If a part never broke, we made it lighter and, consequently, flimsier.[8]

In this manner, they found out what was absolutely needed for the aircraft in order to fly. So, the goal was to make the aircraft, as Albert Einstein once said,

> ... as simple as possible but not simpler.

Simple architecture ...

This is a completely different attitude from what is often seen in software development: As soon as it runs, it is shipped. There is no more thinking about the parts that might not be necessary but are still in the system. This is not a problem early on, but it gets very serious after a while: Although nobody remembers why a part was introduced in the first place, it still has to be maintained and enhanced. So, this is an additional, unnecessary ballast that takes time and money to maintain. Also, the rest of the application has to be regularly inspected to make sure that it only covers the software necessary for the intended functionality. And because

---

[8]Paul B. MacCready, "Unleashing Creativity While Still Getting the Job Done" (OOPSLA 1998, Vancouver, British Columbia, Canada, 1998).

everybody has to rely on the architecture, it must be understood by everyone on the team.

Make sure that the architecture does not consist of a bunch of elegant, abstract frameworks that are not useful to anybody. The architecture has to serve the needs of the domain teams. The architecture team has to get accustomed to the idea that it has to serve its customers (the domain teams) and not just tell them what is good for them. Therefore, it is better to stop developing the architecture sooner rather than later. Of course, a kernel that proves the system can be built has to be provided. This is most often produced by the starting team. Any further architectural requirements should later on only be requested by the domain teams. Otherwise, risks are high that you will end up with either a complicated architecture that is not useful or with a "curriculum vitae based architecture" (an architecture the developers create by secretly introducing some new technology that interests them).

Architecture As a Service

You will often find in large companies that there are several technical service teams in place. These teams are formed around specific technologies. Thus, you will find different teams responsible for the database, the middleware, and the architecture. These teams' work is mostly vendor-oriented rather than project-oriented, focusing on enterprise-wide selected technology. The project teams, on the other hand, would benefit the most if these vendor-like teams would regard themselves purely as service providers.

The architecture should always be the result of requests from the domain teams. *In other words, architecture should always be a service*. The domain teams should not be forced to use whatever architecture has been created and provided by the technical service teams.

This strategy of letting requests determine the architecture follows the *YAGNI (You aren't gonna need it)* principle from Extreme Programming. YAGNI suggests implementing only what is requested and not making any assumptions about what might be required in the future. The idea behind this principle is that most people's clairvoyant abilities are not good enough to predict the future accurately. The focus of the architecture has to be on simplicity and requested functionality, not on elegance or unnecessary flexibility. The more complex an architecture is, the more likely it is that not everyone will understand it properly, and as a consequence, the probability that it will be error-prone rises.

In order to make this happen, the architecture team (whether virtual or real) is only allowed to build what is requested by its customers, the domain teams. And the domain teams, in turn, will only ask for what they need in order to achieve the functionality required by the real customer. To make this service-oriented behavior a habit at the start of the project, it is important to grow slowly, as I discussed in Chapter 4.

Avoid Bottlenecks

If you want to make progress, you are probably suspicious of every bottleneck that might slow down the team. Although sometimes you might install a bottleneck intentionally—for example, having a single integration point, to avoid conflicts (as I mentioned in Chapter 4)—most of the time, you want to avoid bottlenecks, no matter what the cause. Following are the most frequent bottlenecks found in large teams:

- **Coupling:** The architecture has to ensure that the subsystems are as lowly coupled as possible. Otherwise, a single change may require the compilation of the whole application. As your application grows, this becomes very time-consuming.

  Coupling can be resolved by eliminating strong typing (either by an interpretative or just-in-time programming language such as Smalltalk or by generic interfaces, as supported in Java). The disadvantage is, the type won't be checked during compile time.

- **Enterprise-wide object model:** Do not insist on an enterprise-wide object model. Its value is rarely worth the effort of creating it. The higher the effort of creating the enterprise-wide object model, the more you should question its value. It is probably so difficult because everybody (or every team) has a different view of the objects needed. Instead of forcing everybody to have the same view, you may find it more helpful to support the different views. The problem with an enterprise-wide or system-wide object model is that it creates a lot of general dependencies, not only among the objects but also among all teams. Often, you will find that the model is highly coupled, probably with several cyclic dependencies in place. This usually leads to a general recompilation as soon as something in the model changes.

An enterprise-wide or system-wide *data* model is most often sufficient and often already available, as it is rare to work on a company's very first system. Typically, a client company already has a system (or systems) in place and just needs another system (or a new version) that will operate on the existing data model.

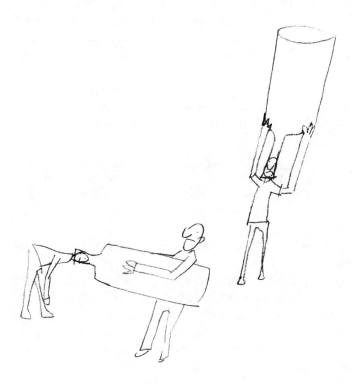

Avoid bottlenecks ...

Although it may not seem so at first, an enterprise-wide object model is actually more of an organizational rather than technical bottleneck. Of course, there is the technical problem of everybody

133

having to recompile whenever something changes. But even more severe is that everybody has to clarify interfaces with everybody else, especially if the object model is closely netted. And besides this, the object model can even be a development showstopper because it often takes so long to agree on a common object model that people will be hindered in starting to develop. This behavior is widely known as *analysis paralysis*.

If you do not have a common business object model in place, one will be required in order for different teams to agree on different interfaces and objects. Make sure that these clarifications are done bilaterally in a pragmatic manner, not a bureaucratic one. As Conway's Law states, it should be a habit for everybody to simply talk to his or her peers without respecting any official communication flows that might have been established by the organization.

Architecture and Largeness, by Nicolai M. Josuttis

Every developer is aware that large systems are only able to scale if bottlenecks are reduced to a minimum. However, fewer know that this is not just true for the technical aspects of the system. If you want a large project to be successful, you need to avoid all organizational bottlenecks.

Agile principles like collective ownership and pair programming help organizations move toward the removal of organizational bottlenecks by helping to support the distribution of knowledge among several heads. However, the architecture itself can also make a significant contribution to avoiding such bottlenecks.

A perfect example of such a contribution is the application of a common object model in a large system. Common business object models (BOMs) are often taught as *the* way to express the associations between all business classes and objects that might exist in a system. They are first modeled by UML diagrams and later implemented by code, where objects have (optional) references to other objects.

For example, in a banking application, the classes "Customer," "Account," and "Stock" would be modeled with their related attributes and their relationships. It is

---

rather obvious, as shown in the figure below, that there are several relationships between these three classes:

- a customer has an account
- an account belongs to a customer
- a customer can buy some stock by transferring money from his account
- stock can belong to a depot, which is a special kind of account

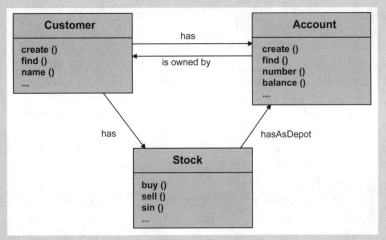

Tightly coupled model

Note that listing even the simplest relationships between these three classes leads to numerous associations and cyclic dependencies. You can keep the model under control as long as it is reasonably simple, but such a system is not able to scale. The problem is that all classes relate to one another. As a consequence, changes will have a global impact (so each team will have to recompile, which can take hours for large projects), and it is impossible to test and develop individual modules because the data types of the related associations have to be known. Moreover, only one or two people will be able to understand the big picture of these complex relations, and they will be the only ones able to develop and maintain the system.

Too often, I have seen bottlenecks like this on large projects. These projects always fail, with immense costs. It didn't matter whether the model was completely designed up front or development started with an incomplete model. Using the former approach, the model was never completed. If development started with an incomplete model, either the model didn't respect the requirements or all domain teams constantly had to react to changes in the model, even if the changes didn't affect their domain directly.

The fatal point is that it is difficult to see the problem behind the problem. Instead of questioning the approach of developing a common business object model, everybody wonders why the object model is still not complete, is changing once again, or doesn't respect the requirements. Besides mutual reproaches, a lot of workarounds will come to existence, ensuring that nobody will ever understand the system again and that the performance of the system will fall prostrate.

The solution to this problem can be described in just a few words: design, decoupling, and layers. Instead of a common object model, the solution is a system with several subsystems (comprehending their own object models). These subsystems are typically distributed over several layers. Finally, it is important to avoid static dependencies in the code. Instead of designing and implementing all possible relationships, the dynamic relationships between the individual objects should be created during runtime within the scope of a business process.

In our concrete example, this means that there will be one module for each of the different domain aspects of the system. A module, "Customer," for all customer operations and data; a module, "Account," for all operations and account data; and a module, "Stock," for all operations and stock data. As shown in the upper portion of the figure below, within the scope of a business process, these pieces of data can create relationships with each other.

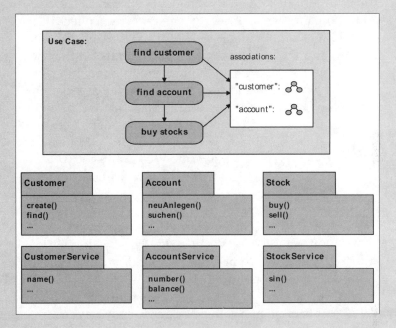

Loosely coupled model

For example, if you want to implement the business process "client buys stock," the client team will be responsible for identifying and providing the client. Afterward, the stock team has to enable the selection of the stocks and the account team is responsible for deducting the price of the stocks from the account (and if required, for storing them in the depot). It is important to note that the common object model is not the central point for the actual coordination. The developer responsible for implementing the business process delegates the individual tasks to the different teams. Additionally, the teams can coordinate themselves bilaterally (for example, if the stock team needs the name of the client).

Using this approach, you will not only get rid of the global object model, but also of the bottleneck it causes. For every business process, individual developers can formulate their requirements for the corresponding domain teams. These teams can then collect their individual requirements and provide the general data types, and these allow the teams to operate on the specific objects. All these individual modules are independently compilable and testable because the associations between the modules are not modeled within the individual teams. Implementing the relationships between the modules individually for each use-case eliminates the necessity to model the relations centrally.

This example highlights several very important facts that have to be respected when developing a large system:

- Tightly coupled systems (including business object models) do not scale. Instead, the systems have to be built in a modular fashion, using loose coupling.
- Any kind of centralism must be avoided. The system has to be designed in a way that makes it possible to realize the functionality in a decentralized manner.
- Cyclic dependencies between subsystems should never be implemented statically. It has to be possible to develop and test subsystems in isolation.

In my opinion, the "meta experience" underlying this experience is even more important because it shows clearly the problem with large projects: Architecture does not scale. An architecture appropriate for a small project may be absolutely inappropriate for a large project. One reason is that organizational bottlenecks play a major role when developing a system with a large team. Therefore, you have to be careful when following recommendations based on experiences with small projects or prototypes. Project size matters—even when it comes to architecture.

Ownership

On a typical agile team, ownership is a matter of trust. This means that everybody on the team is responsible for all the artifacts, including code. Thus, there is no explicit ownership for any artifact, only trust that every team member has taken his or her responsibility seriously. So, whenever an artifact needs to be changed for further improvement, everybody is able to do so.

This leads occasionally to arguments when introducing agile processes—even in small teams. With large teams, people usually claim that this is neither practical nor feasible. Recently, at a talk I was giving, two people in the audience launched into the *classic* debate on this topic. Both worked for the same company and used to work together on a team. The first person argued that she would never trust every member of the team not to screw up "her" artifact. The second person pointed out that without trust, she couldn't continue to work on an artifact when its owner was on vacation or sick leave. The first woman finally agreed that this was an unacceptable annoyance. To bring their argument to a close, I posed the following question: Is it better to comprehend every necessary change to the system or is it more beneficial to be sure that an artifact will remain in the state in which its owner left it? Well, for a start, with a version control system, it should never be a problem to reach an earlier state. By balancing those arguments, those two colleagues agreed that the bottleneck created by exclusive ownership buries a higher risk than the danger of undesirable changes. On the mid- to large-sized teams I was working with, screwing up an artifact was sometimes a problem, but the problems were never severe enough to give up the freedom of making a change when necessary.

Moreover, allowing everybody to change everything also helps to spread the knowledge of the system, which helps ensure that everybody has the same understanding of it.

To further discuss the possibilities of ownership in a large team, I would like to clarify the different kinds of ownership that can be established:

- **Collective ownership:** Everybody is responsible for everything. This is the *classic* ownership model in agile projects.

This means everybody can make every necessary change to every artifact.

The advantage is obvious: As soon as something needs to be changed, someone will change it. There is no complaining about not being able to get a job done because someone else's artifact does not support the required service yet, or anything like that. This behavior reinforces the fact that everybody is to take responsibility for the whole system and not only his or her part.

The disadvantage is, for artifacts that are very central, merging different changes can require time. Furthermore, especially for a large team, you may have to deal with the problem that not everyone will be responsible (or knowledgeable) enough to make the necessary changes. At best, those people will make unnecessary changes, and at worst, they will screw up the artifact so badly that it will not work properly afterward.

The collective ownership model is based on trust among all team members. Everybody trusts that all members will deal with the system responsibly. This means that everybody knows what he or she is doing and existing unit tests detect any potential misdemeanor. However, it will take some time before all team members have acquired the necessary knowledge and the trust will be justified.

- **Exclusive ownership:** The person who creates the artifact has exclusive ownership. Usually, the originator of the artifact is responsible for making sure that his or her work is constantly feasible and functioning.

  The advantage to this is that it is always clear whom to ask if a change needs to be made, and whom to blame if something is not working.

  The disadvantage is that if a change needs to be made and the owner is not available, an enormous bottleneck may emerge. Furthermore, the detailed knowledge about that artifact is only in the mind of its owner and not spread throughout a team. Remember, one of the goals of an agile team is for everybody to have the same big picture in mind and to know what is happening, and where.

- **Team ownership:** This is a combination of collective and exclusive ownership. Every team has the exclusive ownership of every artifact developed by any team member. The team members have collective ownership of all artifacts developed by their teammates. This kind of ownership is similar to collective ownership within small teams, where there is normally only one team. It also has a touch of exclusive ownership in that the ownership is held exclusively by a single team.

In light of the different categories of ownership, you should keep in mind that with the current tools available, you can always have a mixture of ownership types in place. For example, you can ask individuals to be exclusively responsible for specific parts but still allow others to change those parts. For that purpose, the team members implement the change by making a branch, which will then be verified and released by the owner (all supported by the version control system).[9] Thus, the bottleneck is not as big as originally thought. The open source community uses something similar: It has collective ownership for all members of the community, but it reviews foreign contributions before integrating them into the system.

In mid-sized teams, a good strategy, judging from personal experience, is to establish *floating ownership:* Everybody is responsible for everything, thus everybody is allowed to change everything. However, as soon as someone has made a change to an artifact, that person has to take over its ownership. From then on, he or she will be responsible for the artifact until somebody else takes over. Floating ownership requires team members to be able to trust each other to take their responsibility seriously. Usually, you will find that everyone stays in his or her defined *task zone* and is therefore only interested in making changes in that area. Sometimes, a change may be needed in a completely different area. In this case, one of two things typically happens automatically: Either the person who requires the change simply asks the people in that task zone to make the change or the person makes the change and notifies the people in that other task zone afterward. Although both of these methods tend to work out, the former is the more

---

[9]A branch is an intended division in the path of a versioned element (such as a method or a class). It leads to two different versions of the same element.

popular route—probably because people do not want to take responsibility for the artifact in a different task zone.

In large teams, team ownership works the best as long as there is always at least one person from the team accessible to the rest of the project members. Only when an entire team is absent might team leadership prove problematic, but that has never happened to me. Selecting an ownership style that requires trust (as with floating or collective ownership) is a positive sign and an important step for the whole team toward agile development.

Choosing Technology

Technology is a hot topic: One way to market your project is to spread word that you are using some cutting-edge technology. The motivation of the project members is often higher if they know they can learn a lot of new things, especially if that training in turn will have a positive influence on their résumé. So, you will always find several people on your team who would like to make use of the hottest technology available.

On one hand, then, the use of new technology will have a positive impact on the morale and motivation of your team, and on your ability to market your system. On the other hand, running a large project with a large team is already risky in many ways; using new technology will only make it even riskier. As Pete McBreen notes in his book *Software Craftsmanship*:

> Bleeding-edge technologies are great sources of subtle mistakes and errors. To avoid major problems later, the development team must spend time early in the project trying to find all of the surprises, traps and pitfalls.[10]

To be more precise, below are the important risks of using hot technology:

- The hotter the technology, the riskier it is. Chances are low that any other project has successfully worked with the

---

[10]Pete McBreen, *Software Craftsmanship: The New Imperative* (Reading, Mass.: Addison-Wesley, 2002), p. 149.

technology in question. This means your project will serve as somewhat of a guinea pig, discovering the problems and/or limitations of the technology, losing time and money in the process.

- There are no experienced people available, either in your company or in the market. The most experienced people you can get are ones who have read (or written) an article on the topic and have implemented "Hello World!" with the new technology. And despite their relative inexperience, these people will be very expensive because no matter how limited their experience is with the technology, it is more than most people will have.
- The producer of the technology is looking for a guinea pig, and wants to improve the technology as well as the skills of its consultants. Beware—the producer's consultants have never built a real application using this new technology.
- Although your customer believes it would be cool to be the first one using this hot technology, he or she would not like to jeopardize the timely delivery of the application or the quality of it.

Therefore, do not introduce more risks by selecting hot technology.

However, excitement and motivation do not bring this lack of experience in an equilibrium. Thus, be very skeptical of whatever promises somebody makes regarding a new technology.

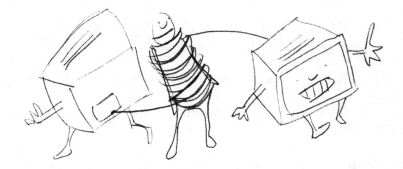

Caution, new technology …

Keep the main goal of the project in mind and only consider selecting a technology that serves this goal—even if it is out of date (but proven). Be open to what people suggest, but make sure they are able to explain the reasoning behind their suggestions (reasons like "just for fun" or "because it is cool" are not acceptable). Ask them the following questions:

- Which problem does the technology solve? Does it create a new problem or solve a problem we do not have?
- What are the two other solutions we will decline because they do not solve the problem properly?
- What if we do the opposite of the suggestion?

Before you decide to use the suggested technology, consider whether you actually have the problem it is supposed to solve, and if so, whether it is truly severe. Also, make sure to investigate other possible solutions—there is never a single solution to a problem. Solutions always balance problems differently; the nature of that balance determines whether a particular solution will help or hinder you. Sometimes, if you consider following a contrary solution, you will be in a better position to judge the suggested technology.

Be careful with proprietary technology. Standards are more likely to survive the time frame of your project, and if you want or have to go for a proprietary solution, make sure that you will have the source code, just in case.

Techniques and Good Practices

It requires discipline to make good practices habits. The better these habits are understood, the easier it will be to make any required changes to the system. The more often project members experience the benefits of these practices, the less discipline they will require, because the project members will start to follow them naturally. Thus, again, it is very important to have rapid feedback on techniques.

In this section, we look at testing first, the precondition for all changes in the system. We then look into the issues of refactoring, which is one of those possible changes. Some of the good practices are best established if the team defines them as standards, as we discuss at the end of this section.

Testing

Regardless of a team's size, it will always benefit from having tests available early on. The most obvious benefit is that the tests, especially the unit tests, provide direct feedback on the design and code. They show immediately whether or not the design and the code work as expected. But they offer even more advantages:

- The tests are the safety net for every further action. No matter how the requirements change, if some regular maintenance is required or if a refactoring is necessary, the tests always ensure that the system is still working the way it used to.
- The tests document the code as well as the design. They describe explicitly the interfaces and their different components. The intention of each of the methods is clearly expressed by a corresponding test.
- The tests show how the code should be used, and they show an example application of each module.

If the tests are developed before the code, as Extreme Programming suggests ("test-driven development"), then they serve as the executable requirements specification. Implementing the tests first leads to a much simpler design than developing the tests after the code. This is because thinking about the tests first requires you to think about how the code will be used, whereas working on the code first leads you to focus on the internal functionality of the implementation. Generally speaking, the earlier the tests are developed, the easier it is to test the system because, according to Eberhardt Rechtin and Mark Maier,

To be tested, a system must be designed to be tested.[11]

However, implementing the tests first is not a habit that is widely spread among developers, but one that is a big change. The minimum you should insist on is that no code will ever be delivered without a test. Thus, whenever something is integrated, it is

---

[11]Eberhardt Rechtin and Mark Maier, *The Art of Systems Architecting* (London: CRC Press, 2000), p. 275.

required that the corresponding test be integrated as well. If there are no corresponding tests available, the integration is refused.

It is likely that after a short while, the developers will not be able to even imagine doing any development without having tests available; they will have become too attached to the benefits to be willing to go without them.

Nevertheless, performing and developing the tests take time, so automate as much as possible. And remember, the larger the team, the larger the code base will probably be, and consequently, the larger the test base. Thus, you have to be aware that running all the tests will take time, because the code size matters. Moreover, the more subteams that are involved in the project, the more you have to take into account that delivering the tests will also require integration effort. Therefore, the integration team (discussed in Chapter 4) should help to ensure that integrating the tests goes as smoothly as possible.

The acceptance tests, which have to guarantee the functionality of the system, need special attention. First of all, they should be developed with the customer, because only the customer can specify at what point he or she will accept the system. Typically, quality control (see Chapter 6) will assist the customer in specifying the acceptance tests. Depending on the system you are building, it might also be required for the developers to support both quality control and the customer, because for some systems, acceptance tests are best developed with code. For other systems, it may be good enough to develop the acceptance tests using visual tools, which do not require any coding. These tools are able to record and later on replay the use-cases. Be aware, though, that developing and running the acceptance tests is normally more time-consuming than developing and running unit tests.

The time required for developing acceptance tests depends very much on proper planning. If you are not able to ensure that the system is planned and developed so that it is result-oriented, and instead aim for components, you will definitely end up postponing acceptance tests until the very end of development. Consequently, you will have a hard time receiving valuable feedback from the customer. Because no functionality can be verified by the customer *before* the end of development, or rather before all the components focusing on a specific functionality have been completed, ensure that development will always focus on functionality. As soon as the customer has decided on the functionality to be included in the next release, he or she can start specifying the acceptance test for this functionality. Acceptance tests should be run after every iteration. Sometimes, you will find that after an iteration, only the prerecorded (old) acceptance tests will be valid, because developing a new functionality could, exceptionally, cover more than one iteration. But after every release, new acceptance tests will also be included, to ensure the successful implementation of the new functionality.

TOOLS FOR TESTING

The testing tools that are perhaps used the most often are the unit test tools.[12] These tools are used daily by the developers when coding. Unit test tools for most programming languages are freely available.

Often, you will find that developing the unit tests is not so easy, because the units under test depend on other systems, like a database or a host system. These other systems are sometimes not available early on, or running the tests against them will take too much time. To solve this common problem, there are *mock frameworks* available that are able to simulate external systems.[13]

It is more difficult to find good tools for acceptance testing. Most of the commercially available tools focus on graphical user interface testing only. The benefit of these tools is limited because the graphical user interfaces are often not the most solid part of a system during development. Because the acceptance of a system differs a lot depending on its focus, a lot of projects develop their own acceptance testing tools. However, there are some frameworks available that are a big help when defining acceptance tests.[14]

I hear occasionally that people are worried about the effort it takes to automate the acceptance tests. However, I have never heard any team complain that making the effort was a waste of time. Systems are more stable if there is a way to run the acceptance tests automatically and regularly.

---

[12]For unit test tools, see: http://www.xprogramming.com/software.htm.

[13]For EasyMock, see http://www.easymock.org/; for MockObjects, see http://www.mockobjects.com/.

[14]For WebTest, see http://webtest.canoo.com/; for Fit, see http://fit.c2.com/.

Refactoring

Typically, if a system grows over time, its design tends to get messier and messier at the same time. This could be worse in a large team because the more people that are building a system, the harder it is to keep it clean. But if everybody on the team refactors continuously (discussed in Chapter 2), the design may stay clean and easy to understand. Thus, refactoring is a responsibility of all team members. However, refactoring does not seem to be a common habit in (large) teams. One reason is that a lot of people still believe it will slow them down. Another reason could be that no tool support is available, which makes refactoring much more difficult than it should be. Another reason is that developers often fear being blamed for not developing new functionality because they are busy refactoring.

However, the most important reason for not doing refactoring continuously is that most people are not trained to do refactoring properly: They do not know how, why, when, or where they should refactor, and they are scared of taking up the responsibility to do so.

Therefore,

- Consider necessary refactorings while planning an iteration (which I discussed in Chapter 4). The business value an essential refactoring provides has to be explained to the customer.
- Coach in continuous refactoring. If the team is used to continuously improving the code, refactorings should not be too overwhelming.
- Occasionally, devote a development cycle or an iteration to refactoring. In such a refactoring iteration, there will be no focus on feature development—all effort will revolve around cleaning up the design.
- Ask the review team (discussed in Chapter 6) to point out necessary refactorings. To emphasize the training opportunity, the review team should not only point out the refactorings but show how they could be accomplished, explaining the underlying purpose of each of the different refactorings.

You should always work toward making refactoring a habit. If you are successful, most of the refactorings will not require any special planning effort. Instead, the team members will start to refactor the design whenever they feel it is necessary, and will only alert you if it requires a longer time frame than usual or especially has to be scheduled in an iteration.

GLOBAL REFACTORINGS

Sometimes, a refactoring has to be accomplished by *all* teams because the necessary change has a global impact. Depending on your system, this could mean that all the teams have to make this change at the same time, in order to keep the system running. Scheduling such a synchronous change is only one of the challenges such a situation poses. Another important one is coordinating all teams and making sure that everybody incorporates the change. This will not be an issue if you have good tools available. These tools support different kinds of refactoring by keeping track of the changes.

However, I once had to coordinate such a global refactoring without any tools. We had to change the interface of an architectural base class. Undertaking this refactoring took us more than a month—we originally estimated it would take half a day. Having gone through this experience once, we thought about how to deal with such global refactorings in the future. The easiest way we could think of was just to resist those kinds of refactorings. Well, we did not really consider that option; instead, we decided to assemble a special refactoring team, on demand, to incorporate such kinds of refactoring.

Such a refactoring team would consist of members approved by the staff association and willing to work occasionally at uncommon times, such as weekends and holidays. Working at such times would allow the refactoring team to make the necessary changes all at once, without interrupting the regular development. Of course, the refactoring team should be compensated fairly for working what most would call undesirable hours.

They will definitely benefit from the support of a version control system (mentioned in Chapter 4). Such a version management tool will especially be helpful if one of the teams is external and has signed a liability of warranty. In this case, it won't be possible for somebody not belonging to that external team to change the existing code or design, because that would require the external team to take over the warranty of foreign code. A version management tool would enable the refactoring team to make a branch on the existing material and later on ask the external team to verify and accept the changes.

Even for a large team of more than one hundred developers, the refactoring team might consist only of two or three members. Typically, it is not that difficult technically to accomplish a refactoring, even one with a global impact. However, a high degree of concentration is required, to not lose sight of the big picture. Yet, it is even more demanding to determine the necessity of a refactoring. Therefore, ensure that everybody can profit from learning about the detection of required refactorings. This knowledge can be spread by using the wiki (if there is one installed) or by publishing the information via an e-mail newsletter. This way, the discovered refactorings will serve as a learning opportunity for every team member.

TOOLS FOR REFACTORING

Refactoring is much less of an ordeal if you use a tool that supports it. These tools usually support most of the common refactorings. For example, if a method is renamed, the refactoring tool takes care that the name is corrected in all references to the method. You will find that several of the integrated development environments provide a refactoring tool as an ingredient of their palette. Some languages have refactoring tools available that are products of the open source community.[15]

Standards

No matter if a team is small or large, its members should all follow the same coding and design standard. This standard is typically accompanied by the programming model, which is a general guideline on how to use the architecture, any specific patterns, and the like.

---

[15]For refactoring tools, see http://www.refactoring.com/tools.html.

If the standard is not met, you have to find and eliminate the reasons for this. Possible reasons include the following:

- The standard is overwhelming. Either it is just so large in scope that nobody will ever read it, or it is so precise that it does not leave any space for the developer's creativity.
- The standard was not defined by the developers, and, in turn, has never been accepted by them. Like the process, a standard has to serve the developers, not act as a guardian for them. Therefore, the standard has to be developed by the developers and adapted to their needs.

The only standards and programming models I have seen accepted were developed by the developers themselves, and were very short and simple. You cannot expect people to read one hundred pages of documentation and remember and internalize the contents at the same time. It is easiest to start with an industry standard and adapt it accordingly if necessary. Therefore, if the standard is not overwhelming but is still not accepted, you have to ask the developers to change it for the better.

These standards serve furthermore as a basis for the review team (discussed in Chapter 6) and could also be a guide to refactoring. Depending on the technology you are using, most development environments provide code beautifiers (or formatters), which more or less automatically impose the coding standard. Such tools can be configured to serve the project's own standard. Some of the integrated development environments have similar tools already integrated.

Summary

To establish conceptual integrity in your architecture, you will need an architectural lead. One of this person's roles is to ensure that the architecture is always as simple as possible (but not simpler).

The architecture will evolve over time and will not be stabilized before the business development starts. Freezing the architecture would prevent its improvement and simplification. Thus, making stable software a requirement, as is often heard, means nothing else than asking for hardware. Software is soft by nature and therefore changeable. This is also true for the architecture.

Cutting-edge technology puts an extra burden on a project. With a large project, you have burdens enough; there is no need for an extra one. So, avoid these kinds of difficulties and question corresponding suggestions. Keep in mind what Rechtin and Maier wrote:

> 'Proven' and 'state of the art' are mutually exclusive qualities.[16]

In general, you have to respect that the size of the team will have a major impact on the architecture. Testing, refactoring, and standards will not only help keep the system flexible and changeable but also ensure that the system will be understandable to everybody on the team—because everybody uses the same good practices.

---

[16]Rechtin and Maier, op. cit., p. 277.

6

AGILITY AND
THE COMPANY

Sometimes it's the headwind,
which carries you higher and further.
　　—German proverb

Large companies often run large projects. The organizational
structure of the companies habitually forces the projects to be run
in a specific way, which gives rise to various problems. A com-
monly spouted philosophy regarding this situation is, "if you cannot change the organization, change organizations." I believe there
are other ways to deal with these issues.

Typically, a large company is structured more by department
than by project. The departmental structure was originally
invented to support the organizational hierarchy and to control the
projects, not to provide the necessary support for projects. Consequently, these organizational departments seldom regard the projects as their customers. Thus, even smaller projects could encounter
difficulties when established in a large company.

This central tension has different effects. One is that a project
will try to ignore organizational (or cross-section) departments. If
this is not possible, the project and the departments struggle with
each other, wasting a lot of time, energy, and therefore money. The
only resolution is to integrate all the departments, no matter
whether they focus on the organization or the project, and to direct
the departments toward the project's goal. But beware: It requires

a lot of time and effort to develop a common focus and combine all the different interests of the various departments.

Typical cross-section departments that are often established more to control than to support the projects are: project planning and controlling, quality assurance and control, audit, and the like. For an agile project, these departments can be very helpful if they work in a service-oriented fashion—with the project as their main customer. In order for the cross-section departments to be an integral part of the project, they have to be involved in the process at the outset.

This chapter focuses on the effect of such a change in the company: the alteration from control to support. For instance, this chapter focuses on how the organization influences the communication structure. We will then take a look at the impacts of enterprise-wide departments on agile projects. First, we discuss how to integrate the corporate planning and controlling department. Next, we look at the effects an established enterprise-wide process has on agile development. On a more technical note, I also discuss the impact of the tools and technology department as well as of the quality assurance and control departments. To conclude the departmental section, we talk about other departments that occasionally interfere with an agile project team, such as human resources, marketing, production, and the legal department.

Then we look at the role of the customer—is it more difficult to deal with the customer on a large project than on a small one?

Sometimes, a large project decides to delegate some work to another company—how does this practice, known as outsourcing, or even fixed-price projects, interfere (if at all) with agile development?

And, last but not least, we look at the individuals working for a large company. What influence does a large company have on the individual employee? And what can be said regarding other (external) project members, who are not employed by the company?

Communication and Organization Structure

If you are running the first agile project in your company, you probably will not have the power to change the whole organization just to support your project. And no project can ignore the influence of its environment. You will have to deal with the fact that your organization's structure does not support the project in an ideal way. If you are able to integrate the cross-section departments early on, they will start to identify themselves with the project almost from the beginning. Often it is possible to integrate those departments without reorganizing the whole company, by just *living* a project structure. The cross-section departments are often quite happy to be part of the project. It is often much more efficient and motivating for the cross-section departments to pull together and serve the project's needs. And the earlier they identify themselves with the project, the better their support will be, because they will better understand its needs.

Such an integration of the cross-section departments turns out to be a big change for these departments. Suddenly, they are responsible for a customer. In the traditional departmental structure, project members often regard the requirements of the cross-section departments as a purposeless annoyance, and not without reason, as the cross-section departments do not always understand that the project members are the ones who formulate the requirements. This typically results in a lack of understanding and communication between the cross-section departments and the projects.

You could eliminate most of these problems by integrating the members of the cross-section departments as regular (temporary) project members or by employing rotating staffs on the cross-section departments, so that members of *successfully* finished projects work temporarily in these cross-section departments.

The established organizational hierarchy defines the communication flow. This established communication flow is often based on linear project development. Because in an agile project all phases of the project could be covered in a single day, and the development is not linear, the determined communication flow often hinders the project. But to prevent the project from slowing down, the organization has to implement better methods of communication. Of this, Enrico Zaninotto said,

> Transmission ought to be direct and not to consider any hierarchy.[1]

---

[1] Enrico Zaninotto, "From Extreme Programming to Extreme Organization?" (International Conference on eXtreme Programming and Agile Processes in Software-Engineering 2002, Sardinia, Italy, 2002).

Thus, the first step is to not take for granted that the organizational hierarchy will define the communication flow.

Project Planning and Controlling

Large companies sometimes have a separate department in place that focuses on planning and controlling projects. At other times, this unit is organized as a project office. The units under plan are components; they respect dependencies but ignore the goal of having a running application that provides the highest business value for the customer.

Planning

Most often, you will find that those departments are accustomed to developing a plan for the whole project up front and ensuring that project members follow the plan during the project. Of course, they have to adjust the plan whenever the project takes a different course than planned. However, taking a different course is seen as a bad sign for the project in this traditional planning approach.

It is common for an agile project to change its course. The course is plotted by the customer, and the customer (like every other project member) will learn exactly what he or she wants during project development. Therefore, the project planning and controlling department is required to plan continuously, which means the plan is not an artifact anymore; it is an ongoing activity. Thus, changing from component-based planning to result-oriented planning (discussed in Chapter 4) and accepting that planning is an ongoing activity are the major requirements for this department.

The project planning and controlling department is responsible for the rough plan. Besides the customer's highest business value, this plan also takes into account the dependencies between different team efforts and risks. This plan serves as the input for the detailed plan, which is developed by the individual subteams for every iteration. The project planning and controlling department then collects those detailed plans and, at the end of each iteration, measures how the estimates compare to the actual achievements. This way, the department is able to figure out the status and progress of the different teams.

Thus, members of the project planning and controlling department coordinate the planning effort and track the progress of all teams, using the tools they are familiar with. It is important to prevent them from including information from the detailed plans of all the subteams. Otherwise, they will be overwhelmed with this huge amount of information.

Controlling

Members of the project controlling function are often not comfortable when confronted with a project that continues in iterations. Such a project is easier for them to confirm that a component has been completed than to verify that the actual software covers the highest business value for the customer. That's the next difficulty: Project controlling is hardly used to working with customers who exert a major influence on project development by continuously prioritizing what should be developed next (especially when this is most often in contrast to the plan). Thus, this department should be reminded that customer satisfaction is the most important measure of a project's success, as Martin Fowler said:

> If a project is on time and in budget, that doesn't mean it was a successful project, but a successful estimate.[2]

Project controlling often fears that iterative projects will continue forever. It is more comfortable with an approved budget, within the limits of which the project will be developed. Thus, as Mike Cohn and Doris Ford suggest in their article "Introducing an Agile Process into an Organization," these fears have to be addressed by wrapping traditional strategic planning and budgeting around the agile project.[3] This strategy is also useful if, for example, corporate planners require one- or three-year delivery plans. Despite the large time frame of the corporate plan, the agile teams plan, develop, and deliver in much shorter development cycles. Whatever the whole team learns regarding progress is fed back by the

---

[2] Martin Fowler, presentation (International Conference on eXtreme Programming and Agile Processes in Software-Engineering 2002, Sardinia, Italy, 2002).

[3] Mike Cohn and Doris Ford, "Introducing an Agile Process into an Organization," http://www.mountaingoatsoftware.com/articles/IntroducingAn AgileProcess.pdf, 2002.

project planning and controlling department into the corporate plan. The produced releases are typically only internal releases, although news of an available release usually piques the customer's interest and the internal releases turn into external ones almost automatically.

Fixed-Price Projects

A lot of projects are accomplished on a fixed-price basis. This affects large companies in two ways: A company might be asked to develop a project for a fixed price, or it might ask an external company to deliver some software at a fixed price, outsourcing parts of a project. No matter if you are asked to fulfill a fixed-price project or if you consider asking somebody else for a fixed-price project, you should take into account the same things if you want to approach it in an agile way.

What does a client of a fixed-price project expect, and why does he or she want the project to be developed for a fixed price? The client feels much safer knowing in advance how much the project will cost. This makes calculation much easier. If we look at the project variables, the constraints of fixed-price projects are as follows:[4]

- The **price** is fixed (of course).
- The **scope** is fixed. Otherwise, the supplier would not accept the contract. The price is typically based on the scope.
- The **time** is defined by setting a deadline for software delivery.
- The **quality** expectation is often unclear. It is not obvious how to measure the quality. The basic agreement on quality is typically that the delivered software has to be accepted by the acceptance tests. (But these are normally not known in advance by the supplier.)

Thus, only quality is open to some variance. Sometimes, during development, a discussion starts about postponing the deadline. But quality variance and postponed deadlines have bad consequences. Nobody is happy when quality suffers. On the other

---

[4]For more on project variables, see Kent Beck, *Extreme Programming Explained: Embrace Change* (Reading, Mass.: Addison-Wesley, 2000).

hand, the software arriving on the market too late could be a show-stopper. Usually it is quality that suffers, as Kent Beck and Dave Cleal note about fixed-price/-date/-scope contracts:

> When all four variables are specified, quality is the first one to go, because it's the least visible—or, it's least visible before the software is delivered.[5]

The major problem for the client is that the scope is fixed. Whenever requirements are changing, it will be hard to incorporate those changes. Sometimes, the supplier might accept an exceptional change, but if any problems occur after the change, such as being unable to meet the deadline, the supplier will always place the blame on the client's change. This will in turn make it difficult to determine whether or not the contract has been fulfilled. If you look carefully at fixed-price projects, you will find that they are always lose-lose situations (and not the win-win situation you expected).

Therefore, if possible, neither request nor accept a fixed-price project. If you *must* work on a fixed-price project, at least make sure that scope is the only variable project parameter, so the customer will know that he or she will receive *some* working software for a fixed price with a predefined quality at a specific time. Although being unclear about the scope at the beginning may sound dangerous, this *optional-scope contract* is the only way for clients to achieve a satisfying result at the end, as Kent Beck and Dave Cleal further explain:

> By giving up the illusion of control over scope at the beginning of the contract, they gain something much more valuable. Instead of getting what they wanted at the project start, they can now have what they want at the project end, after they've completed that learning process.[6]

Ensure that the scope can change in content but not in size. Whenever a requirements change occurs, either prolong the time frame or trade

---

[5]Kent Beck and Dave Cleal, "Optional Scope Contracts," at http://groups. yahoo.com/group/extremeprogramming/files/Optional%20scope%20con tracts.pdf, p. 3.

[6]Ibid. p. 4.

off one (less important) functionality with a similar scope against the new one. Of course, you have to be clear about priorities to make sure you don't lose your highest business value with the deal.

Alternatively, you can, as expressed above, use time as the only variable project parameter. However, quality should never be open to some variance.

Enterprise-Wide Processes

Smaller companies almost always use flexible processes that are defined for each individual project. More precisely, the processes evolve—sometimes into something unrecognizable. Large companies always tend instead to define processes ahead of time, with an enterprise-wide process intended to serve all different projects of the organization.

The idea is great, in theory, because it should speed up the evolution of the process definition during project development. Furthermore, if the process is known and established, it should be much easier for everyone involved to get a good understanding of the status of a specific project at any time.

Unfortunately, it is not possible to define a process that actually serves *all* different kinds of projects, because projects are never alike. Projects differ in domain, duration, people, risk, and much more. An enterprise-wide process buries the risk. To paraphrase Abraham Maslow,

> If the only tool you have is a hammer, then every problem looks like a nail.

An enterprise-wide process tries to develop all projects in the same way, and ignores the fact that an advantage on one project could be a disadvantage on another. The only way you might succeed with defining an enterprise-wide process is by outlining it very abstractly. That could serve as a starting line for projects. Each project would then have to adapt the process according to its needs.

Process and Methodology Department

In large companies, a separate department for developing and maintaining an enterprise-wide process exists, the process and methodology department. As a cross-section department, it is responsible for assuring that the enterprise-wide process is respected by the projects. Usually, the projects have to prove that the process they are using is compliant with the certified enterprise-wide process. Because of this controlling aspect, Ed Yourdon calls this department the methodology police.[7]

Involve methodology police and quality assurance early on ...

If one of the projects wants to implement an agile process, it may have to "sell" this idea to the process and methodology department. There are two big problems that the project team may have to face: The project may not want to follow the predefined process, wanting instead to use and establish its own process; consequently, the project may not be able to present the final process before project development starts, and the process is likely to change frequently over time.

---

[7]Edward Yourdon, *Death March: The Complete Software Developer's Guide to Surviving "Mission Impossible" Projects*, 2nd ed. (Englewood Cliffs, N.J.: Prentice Hall, 2004).

These problems exist because the use of agile processes completely contradicts the process and methodology department's main purpose: It will no longer be able to assure that the defined enterprise-wide process is the only valid and accepted process in the company. Suddenly, a project can take liberties and not follow any established or officially favored process. Even worse, because at any given time an agile team will define the process to suit its needs, there is no real predefined process that it follows. The closest the team will come to that is using a predefined process as a starting line.

If your process and methodology department struggles with these issues, it might have difficulties supporting the switch to agile development. Therefore, you have to find a way for this department to see the advantages of an agile process. A good start is to ask around and find out how well accepted and frequently used the enterprise-wide process is. If it is well accepted and used relatively frequently by various projects within the company, you should consider using it instead of taking the risk of switching to an agile process. If the feedback indicates that the enterprise-wide process is not really acknowledged, you will encounter the same initial situation that I typically do. My findings show that the following kinds of processes can be found in a typical software organization:

- **Official:** This is often the process marketed by the process and development department, and as such, it is frequently the enterprise-wide process. This process is often ignored, despite the fact that the company puts a lot of effort into developing and marketing this process.
- **Perceived:** This is the process that the team makes everybody believe it is following. Some team members might even believe that they are following this approach when in fact they are using another one.
- **Actual:** This is the process the teams are actually using. Sometimes people talk about their actual process as a *no process*. They do not recognize the process at all—they have shaped it in a way that serves them perfectly. Thus, the team members just naturally use what supports them best and eliminate what constrains them.

Ultimately, only the actual process plays a role in practice. All the others exist only theoretically.

One problem I have encountered is that the process and methodology department is often ignored by the project teams. Team members sometimes doubt that members of the methodology department know anything about software development at all, having been barely recognized as developers on any projects. Some take this a step further and believe that the members of the methodology department invent useless processes.

Seldom will you find that members of the methodology department are unaware of this disappointing situation. You can actually use this reality to convince them to accept an agile approach: An unsatisfactory situation is always a good precondition for a change. The best starting point for applying this change is if the members of the process and methodology department work occasionally for a specific amount of time on a regular project. This way, they are actively marketing the concepts of their department on the projects and they are able to exchange their experiences on the projects with their peers in the process and methodology department. This exchange especially allows them to define a realistic (meaning *adaptable)* process and to provide the necessary support for their customers (the project teams).

Until this rotation between project and department is established, you can maximize the mutual support by active integration: For example, the agile project uses the defined process of the process and methodology department as a starting line and adapts it over time. If this suggested process is very rigid, you will have to make major changes right at the beginning. When adapting the process, do not forget to involve the members of the process and methodology department so they can offer their support. Another possibility is to invite the members of the department to the retrospectives or at least to inform them regularly about the outcomes of the retrospectives.

No matter how you solve the problem, ensure that the people from the process and methodology department (the process engineering team) are not separated from the software engineering team. Basically, this advice applies to all cross-section departments. Even if this separation formally exists, you should act as if it doesn't.

Formation of a Process

You may have the impression that the process and methodology department will always have difficulties with agile processes because it questions the departments. But it could also be the other way around: These departments may want to use agile processes as an enterprise-wide process.

As with all other cross-section departments, the process and methodology department must change its self-conception to that of a service provider. The members of the department gather their experiences on different projects and convert them into one or several processes. These processes then serve as a starting point for new projects. The department then has to ensure that project members understand their task to adapt the process to their needs, without blindly following the suggested process. As I discussed earlier, a rotation of members between projects and their cross-section department will greatly aid the adaptation of processes.

Certification and Adaptation of a Process

Since the ISO 900x wave, many enterprise-wide software development processes have been certified. A *certified* software development process is not necessarily the opposite of an agile process, provided that the certification does not result in stagnation.

However, as Monika Bobzien points out,

> Certification leads most often to paralysis. Certification only records the status quo. But innovations do not evolve by sticking to something. Innovations evolve by breaking rules.[8]

Every so often, the people who pass the certification are so happy to finally manage it that they never want to touch the material again. This is when stagnation sets in. Stagnation is of course not the intention behind certification. Instead, the process of realizing and verifying must continue, and people must not stop with a sigh of relief after the certification is achieved.

---

[8]Personal communication with Monika Bobzien, management consultant and TQM ISO 9000 auditor.

It is easy to change a certified process if it has been developed with the knowledge that the world can change or that the process will need to be tailored. Otherwise, the effort needed to make a change is so high that nobody will ever attempt it.

Furthermore, according to author Christine Demmer, ISO 900x certification guarantees neither the quality of the process nor the quality of its outcome—the software application, for instance.[9] Certification only guarantees that each and every step is documented, without any qualifying information as to whether, for example, a particular step truly supports the quality of the outcome.

An agile process needs to be adapted to the individual needs of a project. And projects are never alike. They differ in size, team, skill, technology, domain, and so on. Moreover, projects often need different kinds of process support over the different stages of development, and a standardization does not provide this freedom, trying instead to, well, *standardize* everything.

The necessity of process adaptation implies that there is no such thing as an unchanging enterprise-wide process, and it is ultimately impossible to define a process at the beginning of the project. The process itself will change over the duration of a project, and only at the end of the project can it be finalized.

Regular retrospectives are a good means to measure the progress of the project. But this is not the only purpose of the retrospectives—it is even more important to use them to reflect on the current level of support for the process. This reflection should address the question of whether the process still serves the project at an optimum level. The insight gained from this reflection should be used to improve the process and adapt it to the current state and needs of the project.

When improving the process, you have to remember not only to add new things, but also to eliminate any inefficiencies. A common trap of standards and rules is that there is always a well-defined way to add items, but there is almost never a description of how to get rid of unnecessary rules or guidelines (see Tom DeMarco's book *Slack*).[10] Fewer problems will pop up if the certi-

---

[9]Christine Demmer, "Guetesiegel fuer fleissiges Aufschreiben" ("Mark of Quality for Busy Documenting"), *Sueddeutsche Zeitung, Bildung und Beruf,* No. 40, 16/17 (February 2002), p. V1/15.

[10]Tom DeMarco, *Slack: Getting Past Burnout, Busywork, and the Myth of Total Efficiency* (New York: Broadway Books, 2001).

fied process is defined on a more abstract level. If the process is certified as a framework, it can be implemented in different ways without any need to change the process documentation.

Sometimes, you will be confronted with the question of how agile processes can be combined with the Capability Maturity Model (CMM). According to author Hillel Glazer, there is no conflict between CMM and agile processes.[11] Agile processes are software *development* methodologies, whereas the CMM is a software *management* methodology. Both CMM and agile processes can, and should, be tailored according to the project's needs. So, instead of conflicting with each other, they actually complement each other. In fact, several studies—including those done by Hillel Glazer, Mark Paulk, and Ron Jeffries—conclude that some agile processes can even be tailored in order to satisfy up to CMM level five.[12]

Enterprise-Wide Tools and Technology

Large companies often decide to use enterprise-wide tools and technologies in order to simplify things. For instance, a support department could act as a single interface with the provider, giving first-level support for the tools. Furthermore, this department could help establish the knowledge required to use the tool or technology, providing coaches or training courses. Of course, another important reason for selecting enterprise-wide tools is that it's less expensive when the enterprise orders hundreds of them instead of having each project team order just a few copies. Furthermore, it eliminates the burden on every project team to evaluate different kinds of tools and technologies, which may be quite time-consuming.

Like enterprise-wide processes, enterprise-wide tools and technologies are not appropriate for all projects. Most of the time, they are oversized. The reason for this is simple: The tools department has to look for a tool that can serve all the company's needs. This usually ends up being a general-purpose tool, one that is much too complex and serves everything satisfactorily—but nothing particu-

---

[11]Hillel Glazer, "Dispelling the Process Myth: Having a Process Does Not Mean Sacrificing Agility or Creativity," *Crosstalk* (November 2001), pp. 27–30.

[12]Hillel Glazer, loc. cit.; Mark C. Paulk, "Extreme Programming from a CMM Perspective," *Proceedings of the XP Universe 2001*, Chicago, 2001; Ron Jeffries, "Extreme Programming and the Capability Maturity Model," *XP Magazine*, http://www.xprogramming.com/xpmag/xpandcmm.htm, 2000.

larly well. Consequently, project teams often ignore the enterprise-wide decisions and *illegally* use their own tools. You will often find different kinds of freeware tools in projects, instead of the official ones. However, another, much more worrisome, situation arises when team members decide to use pirated software.

Ask the members of the tools department to support the project members on their tool selection. Do not insist on the enterprise-wide tools, however, because the wrong tool might hinder the team's progress. Often, you may be surprised to learn, the tools the project team requires are much cheaper than the ones selected by the tools department. In fact, the tool of choice is usually a free-ware tool. So this is less a question of direct costs than of indirect costs. The indirect costs evolve if you still want the people in the tools department to be knowledgeable in the tools used. They have to learn another tool, but this will help them support the next project team with its evaluation process.

In one project I worked on, the tools department selected a development tool. But this tool was oversized for the project and, even worse, it was especially good at creating user interfaces, a feature the project did not need at all. This situation was demotivating for both sides: Team members felt the tools department was not supporting them and, in turn, ignored the selected tool. So, each developer had his or her own development environment. The tools department, on the other hand, was convinced that it was doing its best to support the developers. However, members of the tools staff saw that nobody valued their work, even though they chose one of the best (and most expensive) tools on the market. Failing to convince the developers to use the tool, the tools department had to look for another development environment. I could hardly stop staff members from making the same evaluation they did the last time. But eventually, I convinced them to actually ask their customers—the developers. Although this approach seemed ridiculous to some at first, they finally followed my advice, ultimately selecting a much cheaper, more appropriate tool for the team.

For projects, it is often not very easy to find an adequate development environment. The biggest problem is typically that the company has made a strategic decision for specific tools. Often, the expectations for these tools are very high, and so are the expenditures. However, the expectations are rarely fulfilled, and this is not politically easy to admit. Perhaps the tools once did fulfill the expectations, but their quality changed over time. For instance, a later version of a product might be much better or worse than an earlier one. So, it is sometimes the case that later versions of tools do not help us get rid of development issues, but instead intensify them (or add new ones). The project has to address the challenge, question the strategic decisions, and bring about new project-specific decisions.

Keep in mind that the most common problem in software development is a lack of communication, and none of the tools will help you eliminate that problem. In fact, with the exception of a few (the wiki Web, for example), tools tend to reduce communication. Therefore, do not overemphasize the importance of tools and don't believe in promises, such as that a tool will solve all your problems or make software development a piece of cake. Be open and honest with yourself and your organization instead: You hoped to buy (or develop) an all-in-one device suitable for every purpose—there is none, because every project has different needs. Value your employees more than your tools. No project has been successful or unsuccessful because of tools. If you have the right people, they will always find a way to work with the tools they find the most helpful.

Or, to quote author Alistair Cockburn,

> A well-functioning team of adequate people will complete a project almost regardless of the process or the technology they are asked to use. (Although the process and technology might help or hinder them along the way.)[13]

Listen to project teams' needs. They will let you know which tools and processes will help them best and which will hinder them the most. An additional option is to have the members of the tools and technology department occasionally work on a project. This way, they will acquire the best knowledge about the needs of the project as well as the possibilities the different tools and technologies provide. Again, the major change is that the tools department will serve the project teams and not dictate what is best for them.

---

[13] Alistair Cockburn, *Agile Software Development* (Reading, Mass.: Addison-Wesley, 2002), p. 43.

Quality Assurance and Quality Control

First, to clarify the topic, I want to present to you the differences between quality assurance (QA) and quality control (QC), as defined by Hillel Glazer:

> QA is not quality control (QC). . . . To put it simply, QC is testing. . . . In a nutshell, QA is process oriented and QC is product oriented. . . . QA makes sure you are doing the right things, the right way.[14]

Agile processes put quality control more in the center of development than traditional processes. Quality control is expected to work closely with the customer, supporting him or her during project development in specifying, implementing, and verifying acceptance tests. Often, in traditionally led projects, quality control comes into action at the very end of the project: Tests are typically scheduled at the end of linear development. But, if the whole project is running out of time, it is common for the project to shorten or even cancel the test phase. It is natural for quality control to be cut in this context because, as the deadline looms, there is little else that *can* be canceled. And it is only at this late stage that ignoring the schedule becomes hard to do. This means there is often no *explicit* time for quality anymore. This is one of the reasons that quality has to be an *integrated* element of the process.

On an agile project, quality assurance is part of the team—if the company has managed to switch from departmental to project organization. If this switch occurs, quality assurance and quality control serve the project and coach it in terms of quality, all along the development time. This results in a big change for all participants:

- for quality assurance, because staff members can influence the project early on
- for quality control, because quality control is no longer the last step in the development cycle
- for the developers, because they have quality support and verification right from the beginning, which often implies an improvement in the style of development

---

[14]Glazer, op. cit., p. 29.

With quality control tightly integrated with the project team, the quality control representatives are always well informed about the aimed scope of the next release. Therefore, quality control can start to help specifying the acceptance tests early in the project. There is no need to wait for development to finalize the defined scope.

Quality, of course, means much more than the absence of bugs, as Tom DeMarco explains in *Slack*.[15] In this book, he presents a list of quality criteria, of which the absence of defects has the lowest priority. You can prove this thesis yourself by considering the software you use every day. I'd bet your preferred text editor or Internet browser is not defect-free. But you use it every day because it has another, more important quality—for example, uniqueness: It allows you to do something you could not accomplish otherwise.

However, the absence of defects is the easiest quality to ensure. All the others need to be ensured through direct interaction with the customer. But still, the customer decides how much effort a team should put into the elimination of bugs.

The absence of bugs is typically verified by the developers during unit tests. Having quality assurance now suddenly integrated with the team *during* development can lead to a belief among quality assurance people that they should also supervise all the unit testing in the project. While quality assurance people get accustomed to their new roles, strange reactions can happen, as Dierk König wrote in an e-mail to me,

> If quality assurance would be aware that we have unit tests, we would have to fill out a form for each and every class, describing the corresponding unit test.

Other strange ideas that quality assurance people have had include asking to document the unit tests (unit tests, after all, are documented by the unit under test).

Therefore, quality assurance must communicate with the customer to help ensure that the quality criteria are met in a way that is acceptable for the customer. Sometimes, attaining the highest possible quality is not the customer's goal. So, while it is the customer who has to prioritize the importance of quality, developers have to inform the customers of possible problems that are likely to result from a lack of quality in some (technical) areas.

---

[15]DeMarco, op. cit.

It is important that quality assurance is co-located next to the rest of the team, as this will improve tremendously communication and understanding between the development team and the quality team. Beware, though, that enabling this communication can be extremely difficult because quality assurance is perceived as a controlling, not a supporting, entity. Although developers all want to develop high-quality software and would be happy to accept any advice that might help them produce even better software, the popular perception of quality assurance as a departmental organization, with the purpose of controlling (and, naturally, pestering) project teams, is likely to have a negative effect on communication between the two groups.

The members of the quality team must have good communication skills, as the liaison between developer and customer. They will support the customer, providing feedback so the system is shaped according to the customer's needs.

Departments on the Edge

There are some departments for which changing to an agile process should be of no concern. However, you may occasionally need to discuss and clarify some issues with them. The general principle at work in agile processes holds also true for these departments as well: It is always the best to involve them early on. By doing so, you reduce risk that unnecessary misunderstandings will turn into obstacles to the project's progress. Moreover, the better informed they are, the more likely they are to support your effort.

Human Resources

To my knowledge, there are only two situations in which some issues with human resources might pop up. The first is if team members are unhappy with the way the project is managed and complain about this to the human resources department. Hopefully, if this happens, human resources will get in touch with you (as manager) and inform you about the complaints. The best solution is to talk with these team members (and eventually with somebody from human resources) and ask them to formulate their specific concerns. If they are able to raise their issues concretely, it is much easier to invite them to suggest how to resolve those issues.

Often, it is enough to slightly change the process so that these people are comfortable working on the project again. Retrospectives often help prevent such issues from coming up.

The second possible situation involving human resources is if it hires people you have not asked for and do not need, just because it assumes that you will need more people. The underlying problem here is, once again, a lack of communication. Thus, it is your responsibility to ensure that human resources knows what resources the project needs and only looks for new resources when asked.

Legal Department

You may have to deal with the legal department when it is time to specify contracts that regulate, for example, the outsourcing parts of the development, the development of something for a fixed price, or general negotiations with the customer. Often, predefined contracts are available for such kinds of relationships. Yet, those contracts typically focus on linear development and do not take into account any iterative development or frequent feedback loops. It could be some time before the predefined contracts reflect agile development. (Elsewhere in this chapter, I cover the steps you can take in the meantime.)

Moreover, the legal department may get involved with releasing the system. Depending on the application, it may have to verify the application before it can be delivered to the customer. Those verifications may address FDA regulations and the like.[16]

Sometimes, due to legal reviews, a team may have to wait a month or more before releasing the system and receiving any feedback from the customer. Sometimes, this issue can be resolved by defining these verifications up front, as acceptance tests and therefore as normal requirements. However, the time required for verification before shipment is sometimes still required, in which case, the team just has to live with the delayed feedback.

Marketing

Sometimes, the relationship with marketing is established when it acts as the customer for the project. Then everything that holds

---

[16]The FDA is the Food and Drug Administration of the United States government.

true for the customer is also valid for marketing (more on this later).

If the team's effort is product development, marketing may need to know about the new feature set well in advance, in order to produce a coherent marketing campaign. In this case, marketing is obviously one of the main customers of the project. Marketing people are the most knowledgeable in such areas as which functionality has the highest business value for marketing (and selling) the product. Thus, marketing has to steer the release planning and select the features with the highest business value.

If marketing is steering the project, you have to watch quality very closely. Jim Highsmith quoted one telecommunication manager as saying,

> You can rant and rave all you want about software quality (or lack thereof), but the marketing guys run the world and they want market share now . . . period, end of discussion. My job is to deliver on time, on budget, with the 'appropriate' quality metrics.[17]

Thus, marketing will seldom respect scheduling extra time for quality. It will almost always prefer to have another feature in the system. This is another reason that quality should be integrated into the process.

Production

The department responsible for bringing a system into production struggles sometimes with short development cycles. Often, it does not have the technology or manpower to automate all the necessary steps, and therefore it may need more time to bring the system into production manually. This leads to a delay in customer feedback.

With linear development, this delay is insignificant since production is only required once: at the end of development. With agile development, the production department is confronted with this requirement every three months or so. In my experience, this change is always welcome because it enables the production team to steer the project in a way that makes production easier. How-

---

[17]James A. Highsmith III, "Adaptive Software Development" (OOPSLA 2000, Minneapolis, 2000).

ever, production often has problems keeping up with the release schedule.

Sometimes, the application can be changed in a way that makes life easier for the production team. It is wise to consider this early in the project and to integrate the production department right from the beginning.

The issues involved in changing production sometimes cannot be completely resolved, but coordination can be improved over time. The more often the production team can practice bringing the system into production, the faster it will get.

The Customer

Most often, the customer of a large company is either the company itself or the parent company. This is a completely alien situation to small companies. There is one big advantage to this arrangement, though: The domain knowledge is in-house, even though accessing the knowledge is not always easy.

It is also common, on projects performed by large companies, for the customer to be a group of customers. If this is the case, the project's result will probably be standard software or something similar. The problem, when developing for a group of customers, is that no single customer can be integrated into the project. Even worse, the customers may compete among themselves. This makes it difficult to get a customer on-site—there is no accepted representative of the group. Of course, the project cannot solve these competition problems, but it can ask for regular feedback. Unfortunately, since the customers are competing, this feedback could easily be contradictory and therefore not very helpful.

Moreover, the group of customers may be anonymous. Usually, the number of customers is relative to the size of the project. Often, there are either several customers who are invisible (such as customers for standard software), or there is a community of customers who have a similar interest in the project—but unfortunately not the same.

If these are your constraints, then it is best to establish a surrogate for the customer. The surrogate should be a domain expert who ideally has a history at the real customer site, having, for example, worked for one of the customers before. Sometimes, as mentioned earlier, the marketing department can act as a surrogate because it has a very good understanding of the customers' needs.

Another option is to concentrate on a single customer and fulfill only his or her requirements. As seen many times, the market will accept a system better if it fulfills one requirement profile completely rather than half-fulfilling a couple of requirement profiles. As author Alan Cooper puts it,

> . . . designing for a single user is the most effective way to satisfy a broad audience.[18]

Or, as my colleague Joseph Pelrine commented on this controversial strategy,

> A compromise is when everyone gets what no one really wants.[19]

The Role of the Customer

The biggest challenge is to make the customer (who may embody several persons) aware of his or her role. Often, the customer acts as if requesting a software product is no different from asking for shoe repair. Instead, requiring a software product is more like requesting a tailored suit. You will go to the tailor and describe what kind of suit you would like to have. He or she will show you some examples, to help you decide on your desired pattern. Then, with the tailor's help, you will select your desired fabric. After collecting some more facts, such as your measurements, the tailor will start making the suit. But the tailor will not declare it a perfect fit without first consulting you. The less interaction between tailor and customer, the higher the risk that the suit will not fit.

Developing software is even more complex than making a suit. Therefore, the interaction with the customer has to be even closer. On the other hand, customers of software products are often unaware of the need for interaction. They have yet to learn that they are the ones who are shaping the product—that they need to

---

[18]Alan Cooper, *The Inmates Are Running the Asylum: Why High-Tech Products Drive Us Crazy and How to Restore the Sanity* (Indianapolis: Sams, 1999), p. 124.

[19]Joseph Pelrine, personal communication.

state what the most important features are, what level of quality they require, and what the product should look like.

Explaining the importance of their role seldom helps. In my experience, customers need intensive assistance, especially at the beginning of the project. Only after a few development cycles will they realize what kind of power they have, how they can steer the development, and how important they are throughout the development of the project.

Nevertheless, this role is very demanding. It is easier for the customer to state some requirements at the beginning of the project and simply to blame the developers if the system fails to fulfill the new, changed requirements that they were not aware of. If the customer works with the developers, he or she has to steer the project in such a way that the actual requirements are incorporated in the system. The customer should be integrated from the very beginning.

In one project I was working for, the customer complained that the system never looked the way she wanted it to, so she never accepted the system when it was presented. Of course, this left the developers feeling very frustrated and feeling that they would never be able to make the system meet the customer's needs. Unsurprisingly, this customer was hardly available during the development cycle. When I pointed this out, she denied this. So I took her regularly to see the development team, where she was bombarded with questions. After a very short time, she realized her importance to the team. One time, after discussing some issues, she stated her astonishment in the following way:

> . . . only minutes later, I was able to see the difference. I had never realized what an influence I had on software projects.

Integrating the Customer

Agile processes, such as Extreme Programming, require having the customer permanently on-site with the team. Although I deeply believe in the value of this rule, I have encountered a few problems with it. On one of my projects, the customer was so excited about her responsibility that after a while, she identified more with the development team than with her own colleagues. She then started to implement code, and by doing so, she changed her perspective on the system. By identifying with the developers more than her colleagues, she stopped representing the customers, so the benefit of having her on-site was completely lost. Therefore, you have to ensure that if the customer is on-site, he or she will always represent the customer organization.

As mentioned earlier, with a large team, you will typically have a large customer base. Having these customers work directly with all the subteams does not always work out, because the infrastructure does not allow it. For example, if you have several subteams, all with different questions for the customer, which customer would you assign to which team? This question is not always easy to answer, because the different subteams' questions might overlap and one of the customers might then have to be available for several teams.

On one of my projects, we faced just this problem. To address it, we established a customer office, on-site. Although this meant that the customers were not working at *exactly* the same spot as the developers, they were always accessible at their office.

On the same project, we also learned that the end user is even more important than the official customer. From time to time, the end user had different requirements than the official customer. Since the end user determines the acceptance of the system, it is required to involve the end user, also.

Consultant James Johnson emphasized at XP 2002 that according to his research on application software development project failures and successes, the second-most important reason for project success is *user involvement*.[20] (Executive support was regarded the most important success factor.)

Company Culture Shapes Individuals

Most often, you will find that large companies attract, for the most part, developers of average or below-average skill. In order to enhance skills and, more importantly, to make the job more inter-

---

[20]James Johnson, "It's a New World! And It's Called ROI!" (International Conference on eXtreme Programming and Agile Processes in Software-Engineering 2002, Sardinia, Italy, 2002).

esting and challenging, you must establish a learning environment that makes it fun to learn.

Skills

The reason that large companies tend to attract less skilled developers might be connected to the bureaucracy that large companies fall victim to. Even if a skilled and ambitious developer believes that although the company is so big, he or she can be as creative as he or she likes without anybody high up in the hierarchy finding out, the truth will soon set in and the developer's ambition will turn into frustration.

Large companies tend to pay staff according to the industry standard and not individual performance. Also, a small company often provides less job security than a larger one. Consequently, people who do not want to take any risks tend to work for large companies.

Whatever the reasons, you have to be aware of and deal with the fact that large projects are often staffed with less skilled members. You have to take into account that things might progress much slower than you assume. Staff skill is one of the key contributors to project success, as Dave Thomas points out:

> . . . the real value in software development is added when skilled developers write high-quality, appropriate code, delivering what the customer needs. Methodologies do not produce these skilled developers.[21]

Or, as Pete McBreen comments,

> Software engineering makes us forget that what really matters on a project is the skill, knowledge, and experience of the individual software developer.[22]

If the enterprise has decided to build a learning organization, you will have—according to Arie de Geus, the head of planning for Royal Dutch/Shell—great support for change:

---

[21]Dave Thomas, in Pete McBreen, *Software Craftsmanship: The New Imperative* (Reading, Mass.: Addison-Wesley, 2002), p. xiv.
[22]Ibid.

> The ability to learn faster than your competitors may be the
> only sustainable competitive advantage.[23]

Better educating your staff members is only one side of the coin;
the other is to make the job interesting and challenging. So, you
need to provide an environment that makes the employees ambitious, which will then allow them to have fun at their job and
improve every day. On several projects, I found that inviting project members to report their experiences in a technical magazine or
at a conference was an excellent way of motivating them to
improve their skills.

Providing Training

At different points in the project, there will be a need for training.
Depending on the stage of the project, the type of training needed
will differ tremendously. You will first find yourself confronted
with the need for training after the initial team has completed the
referential implementation and you want to expand the team by
bringing all the other staff on board. You will also require training
whenever there is a technological change—a change in the architecture, for instance—and the whole staff needs to be aware of it. Furthermore, you would like each developer to have good coding and
designing habits, but the review team (discussed below) might find
out that this is not the case; additional advanced training may be
needed. And, last but not least, even if the project is under way,
you might have people joining the team later, and they will have to
learn it all: the technology, the habits, the architecture—everything.
    Bear in mind, though, that not all these issues are best covered
by traditional training, and you might not have the resources for a
training center inside the project. Therefore, you need different
training formats to fulfill the different needs:

- **Traditional (classroom) training:** This is very well suited
  to teaching basic concepts. Basic concepts, such as programming languages or design patterns, can even be
  taught by an external training company. For the basic project-related concepts, you might develop your own project

---

[23]Arie de Geus, *The Living Company: Habits for Survival in a Turbulent Business
Economy* (Boston: Harvard Business School Press, 1997), p. 157.

training material, but this is often difficult because even basic concepts can change over time. So, it will require a lot of time and money to provide training courses that are always up-to-date. However, if it is worth the effort, and you have the required resources (staff, money, time), this approach is easy.

- **Mentoring:** To help a few members become knowledgeable on a specific topic, and for late joiners, mentoring is an ideal training approach. Mentoring also helps transfer project culture and establish a close relationship between the mentor and the person the mentor advises. This relationship usually lasts after the mentoring period is over. You might consider establishing mentoring via pair programming, as suggested by Extreme Programming.

- **Agents:** Assemble a team (possibly a virtual one) of agents, each of whom supports a team. These agents transfer knowledge to their teams, and through interactions with their fellow agents, they foster further knowledge exchange from what they have learned in the teams. This is a good way to convey complicated technological changes (for example, changes in the architecture) to the teams and to ensure good coding and designing habits. The agents will market the concepts to the teams they advise, who will further improve these concepts.

- **E-Learning:** Training is required for learning the basic concepts and understanding the team's culture. But it would be too costly to set this up for every new team member. Therefore, provide e-learning possibilities, which guide the individuals through the existing system. The e-learning course could be provided in a very simple fashion. For example, you could make it available on the wiki Web. Trainees could then comment directly on the wiki Website, reporting anything difficult to understand. Next to the explanations of each topic, you could publish the source code (on the wiki Web). Of course, the trainees have to be supported by peers who answer any remaining questions.

The risk in using training material that does not rely on direct communication is that it might go out of date. You can try to avoid that by assigning responsibilities for the material. Although this might work in some companies, maintaining the training material is almost always put at a lower priority than project development. Again, if you can afford to have team members who are mainly responsible for training others, you will not have this problem. But this can bring another: How can you make sure that your training people are aware of the latest changes? Remember, their responsibility is maintaining the training material. You have to make sure that they are regular members of a normal team, just with a higher priority on course development than on project development.

Another possibility, especially with e-learning material, is to use the training material as a reference for the whole system, for which all team members are responsible. This means that whenever there is a change (for example, in the architecture), it must be also integrated into the course material. As a result, there will be collective ownership of the training material, and developers are only allowed to release something if they have assured that the course material is up-to-date. This works best if the course material is based on the actual code and tests. The course material will then serve as an additional acceptance test for the system. That way, nobody has to take extra time to make sure that the training material is maintained, and this supports the *DRY-Principle*.[24] This principle asks you to do everything just once. So, by not duplicating code for training purposes but relying instead on the existing code (or rather, tests), this principle is respected.

For all training material, it is a good idea to keep some basic didactical principles in mind. For example, provide a logical path through for real beginners with special pointers for more advanced people.

Project members, especially new ones, tend to come up with similar questions. Hopefully, most of the questions are covered in the training courses, but often some aren't. This could pose a problem. On one hand, you want to support direct communication so that everybody can talk to whichever team member can answer a particular question. But on the other hand, you should protect your teams from having to answer the same questions over and over:

---

[24]DRY: Don't Repeat Yourself, as explained in Andrew Hunt and David Thomas, *The Pragmatic Programmer: From Journeyman to Master* (Reading, Mass.: Addison-Wesley, 2000).

- Improve the training material so that those questions stop popping up. A trainee could also be asked to make these updates.
- Post a Frequently Asked Questions document on the intranet.
- Improve the documentation so that those questions are answered.

Unfortunately, these solutions often do not help that much; either people forget what they learned in the training course or they do not read the documentation. But, for whatever reason, those questions keep getting asked. Therefore, establish an internal support team that can answer these basic questions and knows whom to ask for advanced support. This support team can also be virtual, with the appropriate time dedicated to support. Sometimes this team is the same one responsible for the training material.

Establishing a Learning Environment

In this section, we look at the different possibilities of establishing a learning environment. Much can be learned from experience, and a review team can ensure that these experiences will be revealed. After that, I look at how much can be learned from failure, or rather how a culture of failure can foster learning. And finally, I discuss the possibility of individual learning during development.

REVIEW TEAM

In addition to the (virtual) technical service team, you might also consider installing a virtual review team to look after the code and design. All the developers are qualified to belong to this team, which means you do not have to pick specifically skilled ones. The review team provides a great learning opportunity for all. The developers will learn a lot by reviewing and seeing different kinds of code, and those being reviewed will learn a lot from the comments of the reviewers. An internal review team helps to improve not only the code and design but also the skills of everybody involved.

Often, you will see that it is a huge motivation for the developers to belong to the review team. To give everybody the chance to learn through reviewing, the staff of the review team should change over time. Often, the same people will stay together in a team for only one iteration or release cycle. The review team has to be careful not to be too picky because this will hinder the teams from accepting suggestions.

To spread the acquired skills, review team members should define the good and bad habits they detect most often. The whole team can then work on those issues in different ways:

- Somebody can lecture about the topic in question. If time and money permit, you might even consider inviting an expert in the field to talk about the topic.
- Install study groups focusing on the topic, like pattern-reading groups. Invite all participants to come prepared to the session—this will support learning how to learn—and to talk about what they have learned and what they still do not understand.
- Publish a newsletter that covers the do's and don'ts discovered by the review team. The reviewers should serve as the editors. Make the organizational structure of the newsletter as simple as possible: Distribute it via e-mail or the wiki Web. Make sure it isn't too long—half a page is fine—otherwise, nobody will read it. Make sure the articles give examples and counterexamples to illustrate the points.
- Designate one to three topics as focal points for the next development cycle. This means all the developers will concentrate specifically on eliminating bad habits.

Of course, you can also consider occasionally asking external reviewers to inspect the efforts of the team. Sometimes, the outside perspective of external reviewers can give you a new insight into your system. However, if the internal review team understands the job, external reviewers seldom add extra value.

CULTURE OF FAILURE

Besides allowing team members to learn new things, reviews contribute to establishing a culture of failure. Growing up, we are taught that failure is something bad and should be avoided. But everybody admits that the best way to learn is through *failure*. It is, after all, often difficult to figure out why something was a success. But it is easy to figure out the reason for a failure and how to eliminate it the next time around. The reviews help teams to regard failures as a possibility for learning: You experience failure, reflect on it, and change your behavior accordingly.

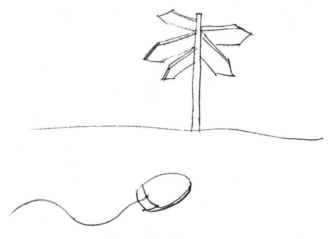

Pause, reflect, correct ...

Depending on the culture of the organization, you might have to be careful how the topics, which are the results of detected failures or bad habits, will be published. In some companies, this is no issue at all; you can speak openly about it. But, especially in companies with no culture of failure established, you might be required to ensure that nobody will be able to detect which team is guilty of which bad habits.

INDIVIDUAL LEARNING

You can additionally reinforce individual learning by using the *gold card* method invented by Tim Mackinnon and his team.[25] The gold card is like a free pass for a single developer, who can use the card to get some free time to work on something he or she is interested in, as long as it is project-related. The gold cards are scheduled the

---

[25]For the gold card method, see http://www.frankwestphal.de/xp2001/Tim Mackinnon.htm.

same way as any other functionality, which means they are time-boxed. Typically, they span one iteration.

Resources

No matter how large the company and the project are, the team is almost never made up of internal staff only. So, although you may assume that the company has enough staff not to hire outside people, management will often find reasons why insourcing or outsourcing is required. When insourcing, individual external resources are contracted, often for the duration of the project. These external resources are always located on-site. When outsourcing, parts of the project are developed by a different company, usually off-site. Eventually, the company will do both insourcing and outsourcing.

Many staff members regularly work on several projects in parallel. For example, they maintain an older system while developing a new system. This means they are unable to devote all their time to one project.

All these different resource strategies can have a significant influence on the project, as I discuss below.

Insourcing

It seems as if there are no large projects without external consultants. Although companies often claim that they want to get rid of them, they rarely do.

External consultants typically provide some specific knowledge, but more importantly, they have an outside view of the project and the company and can bring along their experiences from other companies and projects. This is why they play a special role when introducing change. The main advantage external consultants have over employees is that they are not aware of any political or social constraints between people and/or departments. It is also much easier for them to ignore the official communication flow. They are *allowed* to ignore the hierarchy and can deliver information directly to the intended receiver. It is also much easier for externals to point out unpleasant things. They are not employed by the company, so they do not have to fear the political and social consequences their work might have.

185

Unfortunately, some external consultants have told me that they are afraid of informing management about serious problems in the company. Of course, if management is really stupid, bad news could cost the consultant the contract. But typically, management is grateful when someone finally lets it know what is going badly, raising awareness of serious problems *before* it is too late.

Another advantage of external consultants is that they are relatively unaware of the history of the organization. Sometimes, strange situations exist. For example, for historical reasons, department A may refuse to talk with department B, and vice versa. Or department A may believe that department B is always working against it. Consequently, department A may avoid department B even though department B could provide very helpful skills. One problem with a situation like this is that it is either tolerated ("it has always been like this"), or management is not aware of the situation. Maybe management wonders why things turn out to be much more difficult than they ought to be. An external consultant might ignore the situation altogether, not knowing any better. He or she might just talk to department B, unaware that this is politically unacceptable, although somebody will probably explain this to him or her. A good consultant would then try to find out why, and eliminate the problem. Management has to rely on this kind of information, because otherwise, it won't be able to act accordingly.

I remember a status meeting in which I casually mentioned that I coordinated a specific issue with department X. People in the department I reported to got very upset, because, I was told, they would not talk to department X. They were surprised, then, to find out how reasonable the people in department X were.

Management has to make clear to the external consultants that it wants to hear the bad news. Bad news is good news in that it allows us to make necessary changes and to improve whatever caused the bad news. If the company can't even rely on external consultants to point out problems, it will never know what the problems are. As a result, the staff will be frustrated with the continuing social problems, which will, in turn, reinforce the pattern of only less ambitious employees staying around.

Outsourcing

In addition to contracting many external consultants, large companies tend to outsource some parts of development to smaller companies. The idea behind outsourcing is that you, as the customer, specify the requirements, negotiate the contract, and send the external team away. When the deadline arises, you hope the external team will show up with the working software you wanted. But risks are high that your requirements or architecture will have changed. Both are reason enough for you not to be pleased with the result, even if the external team has delivered exactly what you requested.

Despite this risk, there are several good reasons for a company to outsource parts of development:

- **Specific skills:** The external team provides skills that are not available internally.
- **Faster development:** External teams are typically much smaller and therefore more flexible. This flexibility could result in faster development.
- **Delegating risks:** This is often related to a shortage of internal skills. For instance, technological risks could be mitigated by an external team if it has the necessary skills.
- **Reducing fixed costs:** Typically, the external team is not located on-site, which reduces the costs in terms of space and technical resources.

However, outsourcing is always problematic because the external team's actions are completely out of your control. Typically, it delivers only at the very end of the contract. So, you will only know of any problems the team had once the deadline arrives and no product is available.

What you really want is to have all the advantages of outsourcing—faster development, specific technological skills—*plus* the ability to steer what the team is doing. Generally, however, it would then be more appropriate to develop the project without outsourcing. If you are in need of external support, it is better to insource the people and integrate them into your project team and culture. So, you should always favor insourcing over outsourcing.

If this is not your choice, you will probably need to change the basic contract with external teams in order to take agile development into account.

The basis for the contract is that you, as an agile customer, want to be able to change requirements during development and to give feedback early and often. Moreover, you want to be asked if things are unclear, instead of being regarded only as a negotiation partner. You are more likely to accomplish all this if you work on-site with the external team. This means that if you want to outsource something and expect this external team to follow an agile approach, you do still have to act as an agile customer. Instead of fixed-price development (discussed earlier in this chapter), ask for a system of payment based on delivered functionality. By receiving the iteration and release plan, as well as the deliverables, you can decide after every release (even after every iteration) whether or not you would like to continue the contract.

In summary, following are the major points that have to be considered when contracting an external team to follow an agile process:

- The outsourced team has to schedule its own development cycles according to the ones established by the rest of the project team. It has to deliver to each iteration and release to aid in discovering integration problems early.
- It has to communicate its iteration and release plans. These plans imply the cost and scope of the planned release and iteration. Each release will cover the highest actual business value for the customer (yourself). This means, in turn, that the team must ask you what functionality will provide the highest business value at the time.
- It accepts the coding and programming standards—for example, by providing unit and acceptance tests for its development effort. Furthermore, it agrees to respect the architecture guidelines, which it will help to improve over time.
- It welcomes change, even changes in the requirements and the architecture. It supports different kinds of changes by providing a simple design that can be modified easily. If this is not the case, the team realizes that it needs to refac-

tor. And it runs tests, ensuring that its code does not break after being changed. Furthermore, the team helps to improve and simplify the architecture.

- It does not make any assumptions about unclear things, and instead asks you for clarification.
- It communicates openly and honestly about the status of development.

You can come up with variations, but they should all at least imply the items mentioned above. Often, you will find that you do not gain much by handing out a *complete* requirements specification to the outsourced team. One reason is that the requirements are probably *not* complete—they will change over time, and you do not want to negotiate every little change or, even worse, let the legal departments negotiate the changes amongst each other. Therefore, ask for a specific scope or functionality for each release. Let the outsourced team estimate what the cost will be and sign it off. Depending on the installed project culture, you might even consider not only asking for a specific functionality but also giving the outsourced team the (acceptance) tests that their deliverables have to fulfill. This means the tests are part of the requirements, and that will give the outsourced team a clear measurement of what objectives have been met.

When defining or changing a basic contract, you will need the support of the legal department, as discussed earlier. If it turns out that your legal department will not develop new contracts for outsourcing to external teams, you have to decide either to avoid working with external teams or to convince them to accept agile development. Convincing them means that instead of relying on a contract, you will rely on trust. You might want to consider including an addendum to the contract specifying the most important parts of agile development.

Invite the outsourced team to work on-site occasionally. Eventually, you might even invite the team to work at your site permanently, thus turning outsourcing into insourcing. All of these strategies will enable direct communication.

Often, it is not too difficult to convince the external team to accept agile development because it has probably had some unhappy customers in the past. By receiving feedback often, the team can be sure of the customer's satisfaction at the end of development. Furthermore, team members might be pleased to find out that they are able to shape the architecture so it supports them best. Of course, if the contract is based on components or, even worse, on linear development, you can never be sure what will happen if things go wrong. If the external team backs out on the contract, you will only know at the end of the project what works and what doesn't. So, as mentioned above, this relationship is mainly based on trust. To emphasize that you really trust them, invite the external team members to your retrospectives. This will improve communication with them significantly because they will be much better integrated. They often even start identifying themselves with the internal teams without any special effort. If the outsourced team is an agile team, you should, of course, join that team's retrospectives to learn more about its progress.

The combination of outsourcing and agile processes can only work if the external teams embrace the change to agile development or if they are agile teams already.

Full-Time and Part-Time Project Members

It seems to be typical in large companies for several project members to work only part-time on a given project, splitting their working time between different projects. Often, they have to maintain a system that is in production or they are assigned another, sometimes organizational, task. The idea is to make the most efficient use of the employees' time. For example, if an employee is assigned a specific task that will leave some slack time for the employee, he or she may be able to complete another task during that time instead. But if one of the assigned tasks requires creative thinking, switching between the tasks takes much longer than rearranging a desktop or moving to another office, as discussed by Tom DeMarco in *Slack*.[26] Quite often, the costs of switching between different tasks are immensely underestimated. Part-time assignments have even more effects:

- Part-time members rarely identify themselves with the project.

---

[26]DeMarco, op. cit.

- Often, they use the project support time (retrospectives, training, and the like) for their other assignments. This happens so often because project support time is not considered production time, and production time is typically valued higher than any other time.
- Because they are not in the natural flow of their team, they are often unaware of actual changes. Therefore, their peers have to bring them up-to-date occasionally, which takes time.
- Furthermore, the part-time members sometimes feel ignored because they are often not able to influence those changes.

Therefore, make sure that all project members are full-time project members. If there is no way to ensure this, you have to take into account that a part-time member is not able to spend all of his or her assigned time on your project, that he or she will instead need additional time to catch up, and that his or her peers will, too. Two half-time project members perform less than one full-time member. You have to make sure that the team considers this when planning the development cycles. You also have to ensure that the part-time team member will not miss all the project support time, and that whenever this does happen, he or she will receive all the information later on. Another possibility is to ask the part-time member to work full-time on your project certain days of the week.[27]

Summary

It is absolutely impossible to establish a project as an island in a large company. The organizational structure of the company will always have an influence on the agile project. Of course, you would have the least problems if your company had a project-oriented structure in place.

More often, however, you will encounter a departmental structure that might interfere with agile development. Integrate the cross-section departments early on so they are aware of the changed approach and their required role. By communicating openly and honestly with these departments, you will gain their

---

[27]Thanks to Mike Cohn for suggesting this.

support. This approach is also a marketing strategy. As soon as these other departments recognize the benefits of your process, they will provide better support, thus helping you improve the process further.

Establish a learning environment to compensate for missing skills and to make the job of the developers more challenging.

If you need help from outside, keep in mind that there is no substitute for direct communication. Always try to have your external teams work on-site at least occasionally—if not permanently.

An agile project means breaking with old habits on different levels. Only flexibility in the whole company allows the successful switch to agile development.

7

PUTTING IT ALL TOGETHER: A PROJECT REPORT

We believe to make experiences,
but the experiences make us.
    —Eugène Ionesco

To make most of the ideas discussed in this book more meaningful, I would like to report in this chapter about a large project that decided to adapt an agile process. This is actually an experience report that brings together the practices described earlier.

First, I explain some details about the previous history and the customer. Then, I look at the specialities of the team before discussing the environment of the project by discussing the different departments involved with the project. This is followed by a description of how the project started and then how everything was actually scaled when expanding the team. Finally, I address some remaining unresolved issues.

The Previous History

This project with roughly two hundred members had been under development for about two years when the customer realized there was no working software available and it was impossible to even guess when software would be available. Therefore, the customer decided to cancel the project.

The large company that developed the project tried to convince the customer to give the project a second chance. The developing company promised to do *everything* differently this time. Somehow, this was so convincing that the customer agreed (mainly because the customer was also the co-owner of the company), but with strict constraints. Although everybody was happy about this decision, the developers still weren't very motivated, since they had just seen two years of work get tossed into the bin. At last, with this second attempt, this project became mission-critical for the development company.

Since several million dollars had been spent already, the customer was very suspicious of how this second attempt would fare. So, it decided not to promise money in terms of the full project, but instead decided to discuss financial support every three months, depending on the project's progress. When the project restarted, everybody assumed that after the first (successful) three months, the customer would commit to financing the rest of the project. Instead, it turned out that based on the previous development attempt, the customer decided to stick to the probationary three-month periods. The decision of whether or not to continue financing the project was based on the outcome of each release cycle. Luckily, the team kept on delivering some new functionality every three months. Seeing the system grow reestablished the customer's confidence in the team.

On this project, it was relatively easy to establish an agile process, since nobody wanted to see the project fail again. The limit of tolerable suffering, in terms of finance and productivity, had been reached by the failure, and this had the positive effect of forcing everybody to make quick decisions. The whole company was so desperate to succeed this time that whenever somebody talked about a possible showstopper, it was much easier to eliminate or solve the problem than in the first try. This was even true regarding the bureaucratic rules in the company. Often, things could be solved rather pragmatically, without following, for example, the hierarchical flows, because the project was labeled mission-critical.

The Customer

The customer was difficult in that it was a group of people rather than an individual. To make things worse, this group was competitive among its members, and they were never able to speak with one voice. Sometimes, the reasons for their disagreement were rather subtle. For example, by default, customer A would almost never agree with customer B's suggestion. Despite these difficulties, the group of customers had to somehow work together because they had been merged recently and now belonged to the same holding company. This holding company was, in turn, also the owner of the development company. Therefore, the development company— a typical software shop, whose main task was to develop software for the rest of the company—was a kind of subsidiary of the group of customers. But, of course, the main company was not limited to purchasing from its own software shop. The development company had to compete with other software shops. And to make things worse, some of the customers did not like the project because before the merger, they had started a project with a similar focus, using their own software development capacity.

The customer base chose official representatives who unfortunately did not have enough time for this job. Moreover, due to the lack of a common culture, these representatives often had difficulty finding out what all the different customers wanted. The representatives were also too removed from the everyday life of the end users, not knowing their real needs (a typical difference between customer representatives and end users). This problem lasted until some of the end users had the opportunity to see and work with the system after the second release. The end users were so excited about the system that they decided (also at the developers' request) to assist in establishing a customer office at the development site, where a customer representative was always available to answer questions, test the system, and give feedback. Thus, finally, the end users contributed significantly to the progress of the project. However, many times, the end users had a conflict with the representatives because they didn't agree on the requirements. Most of the time, the problem was that the end users didn't want the complex requirements the representatives requested. This was another reason why the feedback of the end users was so valuable.

The Team

At its peak, the whole project team consisted of 170 people, with 110 software developers. Thirty-five of the team members were external consultants under contract, so luckily the main knowledge was still in the heads of the internal employees.

Fortunately, there were many skilled people on the project, although they were much better educated in the technology used in the first try than that used in the second. Furthermore, there were almost no experienced project members. Many of the project members, particularly the developers, had just finished university and had one project under their belts—the original attempt at this one.

Parts of the software development had been outsourced to external teams, one of which was co-located with the rest of the project team. It was barely noticeable that the co-located team was outsourced and external. Most of the other outsourced teams accepted the change to the agile development process and therefore delivered in the same rhythm as the internal project team. There were several discussions in the preliminary stages of the negotiation regarding a change in the contracts with outsourced teams. But finally, the involvement in the agile process was ensured by a common understanding, not contractually.

Organizational Departments

This section deals mainly with the fact that although the project followed an agile approach, it was not embedded in an agile environment. Like most big enterprises, this one was departmentally structured, not project structured. Therefore, cross-section departments were in place to reinforce the organizational hierarchy and to steer and control the projects. This was the main reason why the departments established for process and methodology, tools and technology, quality control and assurance, as well as project planning and controlling did not think of themselves as service departments right from the beginning of the restart.

Process and Methodology

Within less than a week, I received a phone call that I had been expecting from the process and methodology department. After all, I had been contracted as the process coach by the project directly. Some people in the department were upset and others were suspicious of what was happening on this project. Of course, their main concern was that the project was going to use a self-made process and ignore the existing enterprise-wide one. In other words, they were very uncertain about what I intended to do. Before our first meeting, I prepared myself by scanning through the enterprise-wide process and interviewing several project members about their experience with it.

During this first meeting, I started by pointing out some good things about this enterprise-wide process. Then, I asked them if they knew that this process was not particularly well accepted in the company. I explained that in my interviews, a fairly common response to my questions about the enterprise-wide process was that although most of my interview subjects knew it existed, they had neither seen it nor heard of anybody running a project according to this process. Although it was tough for the members of the process department to hear these replies, they had to admit that this was the truth.

I suspected that maybe the problem with the enterprise-wide process was that nobody had seen it successfully installed, and therefore had no reason to believe that it could ever work. Again, everybody from the process department agreed. I concluded that the enterprise-wide process was missing an example project. I told the process department that I would try to make the project the example that the process needed for acceptance. However, I explained that I would make any changes necessary to make the project a success. I argued that using a process that has never been used might imply some risks or even some inconsistencies. The members of the process department were quite happy with this suggestion, especially because I promised to keep them regularly updated on the changes to the process.

After the project was well on its way and there were only a few minor changes left to make to the process, the process department called me in for another meeting: It had found out that the enterprise-wide process did not seem to work the way it was originally defined. Members of the process department asked if I would be willing to join their department in order to correct it. This was a bit strange for me because at the beginning of our relationship, they were quite skeptical of me. I kept telling them that I did not believe in enterprise-wide processes, at least when they are treated as more than just a starting line. So, I gave them some hints on how to make the enterprise-wide process more abstract and adaptable, by integrating things like retrospectives, for example.

Tools and Technology

The tools and technology department was responsible for selecting all enterprise-wide tools and technologies. So, basically, it was responsible for providing the tool environment. Besides providing the tools, it offered support and training for them.

The current development team had recently switched to a different platform, one that had not been used in the company before (because *everything* was to be done differently in this attempt). So, once again, there was a need to select some tools and technologies. However, this took a rather long time. Consequently, the project members either used freeware tools (starting with Emacs and vi) or they brought in some tools illegally (against the company's wishes). Even so, the missing tool environment was mentioned as the main problem in all of the first retrospectives. Something needed to be done. The people in the tools department gave me various reasons why the evaluation process was taking so long. The main reason was that they were looking for an all-in-one device suitable for every purpose. Therefore, they had to test each and every feature—without really knowing how important these features were, not being developers themselves.

Without even thinking about what I was saying, I asked them if they ever thought about asking their customers—the project developers. I argued that they would know what they needed and were probably quite aware of the available tools. The initial response was a silent but visible shock at my suggestion. I only received support from an external consultant working for the department. But, after a while, they found the idea exciting and therefore started doing it. It still took a while, but the examined tools were much closer to what was needed and furthermore about a tenth as expensive as the ones selected before.

In order to come to a conclusion, I asked the tools department to give one of the tools under examination to some interested developers. I felt that this would accelerate the evaluation process since the developers would be able to test the tools under real circumstances. This way, the developers themselves decided on the tools. The tools department supported them and, more importantly, took care of all the organizational stuff: ordering the tools, providing financing, setting up support for the tools, and so on.

Inappropriate tools ...

Quality Control and Assurance

The quality control and assurance department was one of the first I contacted. I mainly wanted to make its members aware that the team really needed them and that we were requesting their support right from the beginning instead of just at the end of development. Although they were astonished at first, pretty soon they felt honored and understood the importance of their role, which they took very seriously.

However, we had some problems with them. The main problem was that they also wanted to assure unit testing. This, of course, was not a problem on its own, but they wanted each unit test to be specified using a template form and documented. They did not understand that unit tests are mainly for the developers. As with most of the other bureaucratic requests we were facing, we agreed to establish a simple approach first. This simple approach allowed the developers to further develop the unit tests in their own way. The task for quality assurance was to assess this approach for a couple of iterations before being asked to determine if it was good enough to guarantee the quality. So the approach was rather pragmatic: We would do things the simplest and easiest way, but, should this fail, we would switch to a more heavyweight approach. To get quality assurance to accept this approach, I had to argue that the developers would probably stop developing unit tests if they had to fulfill all the bureaucratic steps, which would not have been beneficial in terms of quality for the developers themselves.

It turned out that the quality assurance department was quite happy with the outcome. At an office party, a member of the quality assurance department admitted to me, in secret, that she had never worked with a project that was better developed in terms of quality than this one despite the concessions her department had made.

Project Planning and Controlling

Project planning and controlling had a hard time switching from linear to incremental development. One problem was that the staff was working with a project plan that was based on the plan from the first, failed attempt at this project. That project plan was based on components, not on achieving the most important functionality or providing a running system.

So, only being familiar with linear development, the project planning and controlling team was very skeptical of incremental development and these short development cycles. Yet we were in desperate need of its support because it was responsible for helping teams plan, track development cycles, and adjust the general project plan depending on the outcomes of the cycles. However, the team members were so used to component-based planning that I was not able to convince them to use result-oriented planning. However I argued, they stated their concerns as "we have never seen this working before and therefore this could not possibly work." In fact, this department was so against the idea of switching to incremental development that it had to be forced by the project manager to support our agile approach. However, one member was not as suspicious as the others and was helpful in supporting the teams' planning and reflecting on the development cycles.

After concluding a couple of development cycles, and after the teams delivered some working software in each cycle, even this department realized that the short time-boxes we used in our approach made it much easier to control the project. During a quiet time, one of the most resistant members of this department admitted that although he had thought this would never work out, he had come to see the benefits of this different approach.

Starting Off

The project started off with a team of fifteen very skilled developers. This starting team had technical knowledge as well as domain knowledge. Its main task was to develop a referential implementation within three months, proving that the newly selected technology was feasible for this restart.

The first attempt had been mainly regarded a technical failure because it never resulted in working software. However, this wasn't the full truth, because with better organizational management and a better process, these problems would have been solved without any difficulties. The referential implementation developed by the starting team created the underlying architecture for the system and showed, within an executable application, that some business use-cases could also be realized.

All this happened while the rest of the team, which contained more than one hundred people, was sitting around. These team members had the task of familiarizing themselves with the domain, although they had already worked on this business domain during the first try. Thus, it was rather obvious that this was not really a task but a way to keep these people busy. They were also asked to acquaint themselves with the new technology, and they all observed as the referential implementation grew. The starting team, on the other hand, ensured that everything was visible via the project's wiki Web. This was one of the differences the starting team settled, which was one step toward a new definition of development quality. This quality was defined by the following:

- **Simplicity:** The most important decision was to have as simple an architecture as possible, so that it was understandable by everybody on the team. The chief architect enforced the decision not to use any technology that wasn't truly needed, no matter how hip at the moment. Instead, whenever somebody came up with a new technological suggestion, he or she was asked which of the project's problems it would solve. Most answers were not very convincing, and the suggestions were declined.

- **Transparency:** All decisions were transparent. All information about the project was always visible on the internal wiki Web, so even people who weren't a part of the starting team always knew what was going on. In contrast to previous projects, everybody had the big picture in mind and was aware not only of all decisions, but also of his or her possible influence on those decisions. This way, everybody was conscious of the project's progress and felt responsible for the project.

- **Communication:** Transparency is a quality that is based on open communication. Thus, the wiki Web also served as a communication media. But the most important decision concerning improved communication was to have all team members work in the same room. This was much easier with the starting team, which consisted of fewer than twenty people. Co-locating the full team, however, was a bigger challenge (discussed below). In the first attempt at this project, co-location, or the lack thereof, was a big issue: The team was spread over several buildings in the city, making direct communication almost impossible.

  To further enable communication, we always made sure to have some food available at main spots. People soon began to congregate around the food and discuss the project over a snack or two.

- **Fun:** Not surprisingly, fun and motivation were more or less nonexistent after the cancellation of this project during the first try. Thus, it was very important to celebrate even tiny successes at the beginning of the restart. Although parties are a good way to reestablish fun and motivation in a team, the actual successes are more important. The main motivation came from seeing the referential implementation evolve and succeed.

- **Discipline:** It was essential that the starting team established a development discipline. For example, it ensured that there were unit tests available for every piece of code. It also integrated its deliveries as soon as they were finished. Having these habits in the starting team made it easier to establish them in the full team.

  The system underwent external reviews by well-known reviewing companies, both at the very beginning of the project and later on. Thus, there was not only the need to make the application run at the end of every release but also to make it understandable by and acceptable to the external reviewers. In order to ensure that the project passed the external reviews, the team came up with a coding standard and, much more importantly, with a programming model stating the do's and don'ts for implementing the application.

  Also, all team members were forced from the very beginning to not work overtime and to take their vacations.

Vacation …

The new architectural lead ensured early on that everybody on the team had the same understanding of the system. He was also the one who made sure, over and over, that the team understood itself as *one* team and not as several concurrent teams. In the first try, one of the main issues was that the business people and the technical people worked more against each other than with each other.

Growing the Team

The referential implementation finished on time (it took three months). This was a big success because, for the first time, the team actually delivered. The result after those three months was bigger than what resulted after two years on the first try. Of course, this great success was celebrated with a big party.

Team party ...

To reflect on the achievements of the first three months, the starting team went off-site for a closed meeting. During this reflection, this team decided it would need another three months to clean up the architecture. However, the members of the project team who were not part of the starting team were waiting to start. For financial reasons (having one hundred people sit around unproductively costs a lot), the project manager was forced to start expanding the team immediately, taking the rest on board. Although the expansion of the team was mainly financially motivated, this decision was also very important for the motivation of the rest of the team. Everybody wanted to be part of this successful team and, moreover, everybody wanted to forget his or her experiences on the failed project, which was the only project experience that most of the team members had ever had.

Now that this project had started so successfully, the project manager did not want to risk anything and therefore took great care to create and establish a development process that served the needs of the team. From the starting team, we had the experience of a development process and knew that it worked for a small team. So, we carefully started scaling this process as we grew the team.

However, the starting team claimed at first that it did not follow any particular process at all. Whenever a successful team says this, you can be assured that it is using a process that is serving it perfectly. The process is serving the team so well that it does not experience the process as an extra task. Instead, it just uses it naturally. Thus, the team members just do whatever helps them and omit whatever hinders them. But they never think that these decisions are process-related; to them, these decisions are just coming naturally. However, it is a real challenge to pick up such a (hidden) process and transfer it from a fifteen-person team to a team of more than one hundred people. As mentioned earlier, with a large team, a lot of positive things do not come naturally; instead, sometimes more negative things come for free.

Learning from Previous Problems

Thus, to scale the process, the first thing I did was interview randomly picked members of the project team. The main questions in the interviews, which were always one-on-one, focused primarily on the lessons learned in the first try. I ensured that the lessons learned covered both the things that went well and the things that should have been improved. Interestingly, people were astonished as soon as they realized that although the first try was always regarded as a failure, there were still parts that went quite well. Realizing the good things helped the team members to shake off their lethargy and to feel new energy. They realized that their efforts were not so bad in the first try, after all. Consultant and author Norm Kerth describes the same experience in *Project Retrospectives,* when talking about postmortems:

> Before the postmortem, no one had realized that significant gains had occurred in the department alongside the failures.[1]

But, as is often the case, I received much more information about the things that went wrong and the things team members worried would happen again. The risk that was named the most often was the cultivation of a front line between the technical team and the domain team. Although a lot of blaming was done against almost all the teams, it turned out that the relationship between technical staff and business people was especially bad. Each side felt misunderstood by the other.

While expanding the team, this problem popped up again. For example, the domain teams blamed the technical teams for not being able to rely on the architecture, saying they couldn't rely on it as long as it was still under development. On the other hand, the idea was to allow the architecture to evolve according to the needs of the business domain teams. But, instead of taking their chance, the domain people thought that an evolving architecture would only have a negative impact on them. Moreover, they feared that they would not be able to deliver on time because of the evolving architecture. We did not succeed in selling the new purpose of the technical teams, which was to serve the domain teams. Basically, the domain teams did not trust this new model.

Therefore, we used a trick: We announced that the architecture was finished (regardless of its state at the time) and that the business domain teams could use it as-is. We promised that the architecture would not undergo any further changes. After this, the business domain teams immediately started to develop.

It did not take very long before a business domain team came up with the first change request for the architecture. Rather than forward the request, we established the following process: All the business domain teams discussed whether or not they would all

---

[1]Norman L. Kerth, *Project Retrospectives: A Handbook for Team Reviews* (New York: Dorset House Publishing, 2001), p. 192.

profit from this change. Whenever the majority thought it would benefit, the teams would ask the technical teams to incorporate it. So, finally, the business domain teams accepted the service that the technical teams provided, and more importantly, they accepted that the architecture was not stable, but evolving. Having installed this process, every team (including the technical teams) was allowed to ask for a change. This way, the technical teams also learned to assess internal improvements transparently to their customers.

Another major risk that was often mentioned during the interviews was the fear of decision-making. It seems that in the first attempt, decisions were often either postponed forever or made but not acted upon. Therefore, most of the problems were brought up in every meeting because the decisions concerning these problems had never been taken seriously. Our new philosophy was quite the opposite: We preferred to make even a wrong decision and realize it than to do nothing, until we learned more and discovered how to correct the decision.

There were, furthermore, a couple of technical problems mentioned. For instance, the unacceptable frequency of network unavailability: The team was often blocked in development because the network was not up and running. Unfortunately we were not able to change this, because the network availability was out of our control. However, we tried to escalate problems like this as early as possible, in order to avert further damage.

Although network availability was not a risk that was internal to the project, there were technical problems that were. For example, due to the massive dependencies among all components, the process of compilation, link, and integration took an unacceptably long time. We tried to address this problem with result-oriented planning and with simple design, which helped us avoid such bottlenecks.

The last risk that was mentioned during the interviews dealt with communication. In the first try, not only was the team spread over different buildings, but those buildings were spread across the whole city. So, there was hardly a possibility of communicating directly with other team members. This problem was emphasized by the fact that not all the team members knew each other.

All the risks mentioned, together with the good things formulated, were used to scale the process.

Training

To spread the word about the architecture and how things should be implemented, we started a one-week training course for all new developers. Almost every member of the starting team served as a trainer. This was not the best decision didactically because it was the first time most of the trainers had taught a course. However, they were the first-class knowledge resources, and this way, the new members knew immediately who was the expert for each topic.

In addition to this training, we established a foster program. Two members of the starting team acted as foster parents for one of the new teams. For most of the teams, this worked very well, but for some it did not work at all. The main reason for the failed foster programs was that the foster parents thought it was enough simply to be available. They assumed that someone on their assigned team would call whenever he or she encountered a problem. But this did not happen. Sometimes, team members did not know what to ask, and sometimes they were afraid of seeming stupid. The program worked well for teams whose foster parents regarded themselves as a service provider for their assigned teams. Those foster parents sought out their teams and discussed regularly the status of their learning with them. The foster program lasted four to eight weeks, depending on the needs of the new team.

After this initial training phase, the need for further training was ignored because there were more pressing problems to be solved. However, the lack of training popped up later on. On one hand, this was because some members changed their topics, taking up responsibility for tasks they had not done before. On the other hand, this was based on the success of the project: Having delivered a couple of external releases, other software development projects in the company considered using our architecture as their platform. We favored this new challenge because it helped us to further increase our marketing and spread the word of our success. This was important because although we had successfully delivered a couple of times, there were still some customers who did not trust us and, even worse, often gave us the impression that they would love to see us fail. So, the more people who were convinced of our accomplishments, the less weight the arguments of those critical customers carried.

Foster parents ...

Meanwhile, however, the existing training material was out-of-date because everything had undergone a lot of changes. We decided to develop the training material internally, and to pass it on to the tools and technology department, which would hold the training courses and maintain the course material. The training material itself was built on three columns:

- Traditional slides for the course.
- A walkthrough on the wiki Web. This walkthrough had basically the same contents as the slides (which were also available on the Web) but with some additional information and even links to more advanced topics. Thus, the wiki Web served more for self-learning.
- Source code that showed everything covered by the training course and that was also available on the wiki Web.

The slides were maintained by the tools and technology department. The other two were under the collective ownership of the development team. So the walkthrough and the example source code were used not only in training but also as a reference for the system. The whole team had to ensure, whenever it made any changes to the system, that the source code used in the training material still worked and that the walkthrough was still valid.

Thus, running the training material's source code was yet another acceptance test of the system. However, the team had to be regularly reminded to ensure the validity.

Establishing Short Iterations

The results of the interviews served as a starting point for our scaled agile development process. It turned out that implementing very short development cycles was extremely important. We established release cycles lasting three weeks, each consisting of three one-week iterations. The goal of each release cycle was some additional useful functionality for the customer.

One of the main arguments for installing short iterations was that we wanted to be able to correct mistakes as early as possible. Only a closed release cycle, which is a cycle that lasts for a defined time and concludes with a specified outcome, gave us the possibility of evaluating the system under development. Insisting on an always-running system helped us detect major issues right at the beginning, such as integration, how to implement acceptance tests, and how to bring the system into production. We preferred to solve these issues while the system was rather small, and we could try different approaches, rather than to address the issues later on, when the system was already big.

We started the first cycle with guided planning workshops. It turned out that it was possible to lead five teams in a planning workshop at once. To set the stage, I gave the teams some background information about the purpose of short and time-boxed release cycles. Moreover, I explained the relationship between the four project parameters (resources, time, quality, and scope) and added that for this project, we would use scope as the only variable parameter. This way, we wanted to avoid any decrease in quality. Only the first two planning sessions needed guidance. Thereafter, the teams did the planning on their own and reported the outcome to project planning and controlling, as well as to quality assurance.

The major experience of introducing short development cycles was that we stuck to the time-box. At first, the short duration of these cycles was a shock for almost everybody. Most team members ignored this change at first, and it took them more than a week just to get started. Those people trusted their experience that in this large company, things always took much longer than people said. But as soon as they realized that the deadline would not change, they got up to speed even though half of the release cycle had already passed. However, at the same time, they started complaining about how unfair it was that the release cycle now only covered half of the assumed time. Moreover, they doubted that it was possible to complete anything in this short time frame.

It was very important to keep the cycles time-boxed and to meet the deadline. This was the only way to emphasize that sticking to the time-box was something we all took seriously. We wanted to make sure that we did not fall into the trap Fred Brooks describes in *The Mythical Man-Month:*

> How does a project get to be a year late? . . . One day at a time.[2]

Learning to Reflect

Right after the first iteration, I invited all of the team leaders to reflect on it. Moreover, after finishing the first release cycle, I scheduled a retrospective on the process we had used so far. These retrospectives became the most important and popular meetings. They also served as a forum for the exchange and discussion of problems among peers and, later on, for the discussion and coordination of new architectural requirements. So, retrospectives became *the* forum for the developers. Although everybody eventually came to value this forum later on, it did not work quite so smoothly at first. For example, a typical situation was one in which a team talked about its problems, but no other team voiced similar concerns. At such a point, people were not willing to exchange their problem-solving strategies. It was clear that the different teams did not yet realize that they were all parts of one single team that should support each other instead of watching each other fail. Whenever this happened, I would comment that it seemed doubtful that no other team had encountered the same problem and found out what worked and what didn't in solving it. Typically, following my comments, one of the other teams would start talking about how they solved the problem.

---

[2]Frederick P. Brooks, Jr., *The Mythical Man-Month: Essays on Software Engineering,* 20th anniv. ed. (Reading, Mass.: Addison-Wesley, 1995), p. 153.

All retrospectives were further accompanied by project planning and controlling, as well as by the quality assurance department.

Enabling Communication

One of the main reasons the starting team was successful was based on the decision to co-locate it. But now, as I mentioned earlier, we faced the challenge of co-locating more than one hundred people. This problem was actually considered one of the project's biggest risks for a while, although it was partially solved over time.

We soon managed to occupy one whole open-plan office, using the flexible workplace concept I described earlier in the book. This partially solved the problem, but shortly after, almost everybody realized that all the project knowledge was located in this open-plan office. As a consequence, every morning brought a big run of team members to get a seat in this office—so they wouldn't miss any important information. Whoever was sitting there could be sure to know what was going on, whereas at other places, information came the traditional way—slowly and filtered, via e-mail, for instance.

However, we finally solved this problem by occupying an open-plan office next to the first one. Together, the two offices provided enough space for almost everyone. This allowed us to ensure that team members could sit together, which had a tremendous effect on poorly performing teams. As soon as the whole subteam was able to sit together, it performed much better. Furthermore, the flexible workplace philosophy helped us because whenever two teams seemed to not get along with each other very well, we moved them next to each other so they became aware of each other's problems, which in turn led to a much better understanding. By co-locating teams whenever necessary, we solved most of these communication problems. This applied not only to development teams, but also to teams such as project planning and controlling and quality assurance.

Of course, not all communication problems could be solved by co-location. Besides retrospectives, we established two more information channels with a mainly one-way information flow. Both were plenary meetings: one for everybody who was somehow related to the project and one for developers only. Whenever one of the developers felt the need to spread the word about some newly gained information, he or she would announce one of these developer-only meetings. Generally, such a meeting was scheduled every week but would only take place when there was some information to pass on.

Flexible workplace ...

We addressed other communication problems by installing an explicit communication structure. We had different people visit the teams regularly to check up on them and their problems. These team visitors were useful for passing information, but also, more importantly, for gaining awareness of the problems of the individual teams. However, it was not enough simply to collect those problems; they had to be addressed, which was the additional task of those team visitors. This did not mean that the team visitors were directly responsible for solving all problems, but they were expected to facilitate the solution by, for example, bringing the right people together. In this way, the team visitors acted as communication managers.

There were different team visitors, and some of them changed over time, depending on the major problems of the project. For instance, in the beginning, it was primarily only me visiting the teams. Although I mainly focused on getting hints for better-adapting the process, I also discovered and addressed other problems. Later on, we had additional team visitors, from the technical service teams who focused on the architecture. They helped the teams adjust to new changes in the architecture and checked back with the teams on how the architecture could serve them better. Finally, the last team visitors were members of the virtual review team, whose main focus was reviewing the teams' accomplishments. All team visitors had the additional task of listening to all kinds of problems, whether they were related to the visitors' main focus or not.

Of course, we also had the more traditional communication channels in place: e-mail and phone. The wiki Web served not only as a discussion medium but also as a medium for knowledge transfer. However, these more traditional communication channels became problematic, whenever they were too successful and therefore overused: For example, e-mail was not read if one was receiving too many e-mails every day. The wiki Web was difficult to read once too much information became available there and it became too complex. Communication is always a challenge.

Managing Outsourced Teams

Parts of the development had been outsourced to external teams. The decision to do this was made early on, but most of the contracts had still not been finalized as the rest of the team entered the second development cycle. Having seen the internal teams successfully follow an agile approach, everybody felt the need to ask the outsourced teams to also accept this process. Furthermore, the whole set-up already implied this approach—for example, the idea of an evolving architecture made impossible the use of a linear approach. However, there was no way to change the basic legal contract. This would have taken another year or so. Therefore, we decided to come up with a little pamphlet explaining our strategy and what we expected from the outsourced teams. This pamphlet was delivered as an appendix to the contract.

For some external teams, it was no problem at all to switch to an agile approach, because they had been co-located at our site, anyway. Thus, they were not outsourced teams in the classical sense, but almost insourced teams. This way, they had seen the internal teams changing the process and had started automatically to use the same process. However, it was much more difficult convincing some of the other external teams to accept our strategy. Firmly believing that actions speak louder than words, we invited them to the planning workshops and the retrospectives. They found both gatherings helpful, especially the retrospectives, which they felt were a great forum to retrieve all relevant information and to give feedback.

Unresolved Issues

Despite the success, there were a couple of things that did not work out so well, mainly because of changes that the teams refused to make. However, because the project was still a success overall, maybe we should not look at these as *unresolved issues,* because they did not prevent the project from succeeding. On the other hand, if the desired changes had been made, some problems would have been eliminated and, therefore, certain parts of the project would have gone much smoother.

You should always respect the limitations of asking for change. If the team refuses to make a change, you have the following options:

- You can force the team to accept the changes, but you can be pretty sure that the resistant members of the team will always find a way around them or, even worse, will find a subtle way to undermine those changes in order to prove they do not work.
- You can put the change on hold, knowing that it may well be on hold forever. You are left to hope that the time will come when you can find—together with the team—the perfect way to introduce this change.
- You can decide to get rid of the whole team. Most likely, you will be the one to leave the team in order to execute

this decision. Another possibility is that there are only a few members on the team who are resistant to the changes. If this is the case, you might be able to get rid of them. Unfortunately, though, this is not very likely—often, the resistant people are highly skilled and have support from project management.

On my team, we decided to put two changes on hold. One was to plan development cycles according to functionality and not components—there was no way of convincing *all* the teams to do this. The "component-based teams" received very good support from the project planning and controlling department, which favored component-based planning because it is more common with a linear approach and was easier to reflect in the department's planning tool. Thus, it occasionally happened that some of these teams needed three or more release cycles before they delivered some functionality that could be acceptance tested.

The other change we put on hold was to establish a culture of responsibility. Although the team members said that they would take responsibility for assigned (or volunteered) tasks, they regularly had difficulties bearing the responsibility. For example, as soon as something did not work out, it did not occur to them to look for the problem somewhere else and work on a solution there. Instead, they started complaining that they were not able to fulfill their assigned task because they did not have everything they needed in order to proceed. This lack of responsibility was definitely a serious issue, and team visitors were told to ask the team members how they were progressing with the tasks they were responsible for. However, this strategy of following up did not help to build a culture of responsibility, because the team visitors assumed the responsibility in the end. This reinforced the idea that there will always be somebody who will be able to look further than you in search of an answer to your problem.

Summary

When I talked to colleagues about this project, a lot of them said they would have liked to work on a project like this, that it sounded like fun. They were right—it was a lot of fun to work on this project—but it was not so much fun at the beginning. We had to work very hard to convince everybody that it was one, single project and that we could only succeed if we all worked together.

My feeling is that there is a deep relationship between the willingness to change and the experience of having failed before. I am pretty sure that a lot of changes would have been almost impossible to introduce if this project was not a second attempt at a failed project. People are generally more open to change when they have reached their own limit of suffering in their old habit. Before they reach this limit, they will do things as they have always done. So, the fact that the failure of the first attempt brought almost everyone involved to his or her limit of suffering helped teams to work in a more pragmatic way with other departments, external teams, and the customer. However, I do not recommend that you

plan to throw one away; you will, anyhow.[3]

as Brooks writes in *The Mythical Man-Month*. Instead, I recommend that you remain open to change, even if things are not that bad, and that you give new approaches a try before condemning them.

---

[3]Brooks, op. cit., p. 116.

AFTERWORD

Believe nothing,
no matter where you read it,
or who said it,
no matter if I have said it,
unless it agrees with your own reason
and your own common sense.
　　　　—Gautama Siddharta Buddha

When reflecting on different success factors, I lean more and more to the conclusion that it all comes down to communication and continuous feedback. Although feedback can be obtained technologically, via tests and the like, it seems to be more important to obtain personal feedback from teams and individual project members. Retrospectives are a great means for this exchange. However, I have learned the most by speaking directly with individual project members. The roots of problems often have so many facets, which (along with their corresponding solutions) are well known by the people most of the time but are badly expressed (if at all). In order to succeed, this knowledge has to be uncovered by the change agent.

Another important point that occurs to me is that stability is much more negative than it is thought to be. Whenever somebody asks me to stabilize something—for instance, the process or the architecture—I wonder why I am being asked to help this thing die. As long as we are allowed to learn, things will change and therefore they will not be stable.

Sometimes, when I learn something, I feel that something else has to change. However, making this change occasionally requires me to break rules. Rules should never hinder you from changing something for the better, although this means you have to be courageous and sometimes take a difficult path. Often, processes are so well-laid-out, especially in large companies, and so many options are completely ruled out, that it seems impossible to break through. But it is only impossible if you do not try.

For some reason, people assume that a large project has to be performed in a more formal, rigid, and heavyweight fashion than a small project. In my experience, it is crucial not to over-specify the process or bog it down with too many rules. Maybe this is because I am most often so busy coordinating the individual subteams. I typically let the subteams decide what kind of internal team development process they want to use. I believe that if I were to start specifying the process for each and every subteam, I would need a process coach for each of them. Therefore, I concentrate on the agility of the overall project with respect to individuals over processes.

On a small project, people tend to trust their common sense and their gut feeling. However, all software problems are people problems, whether they occur on a large project or a small one. That is why agile methodologies focus on the human aspect. Thus, generally speaking, all agile methodologies, scaled or not, are about attitudes toward change and attitudes toward people. But every person and every team is different, and these differences must be respected when requesting specific changes.

In this book, I have described *my* best practices for applying agility to large projects. However, these are not recipes—what works well for me and some of my colleagues will not necessarily work for you. Thus, if you discover that one of the presented practices does not work for you, analyze its objectives first; then consider the importance of these objectives for your project. If you still believe that they are important, you will have to find another approach that will help you reach your goals. The important thing is the value system that is carried by these practices. Other than that, even when dealing with a large project, the most important thing is to follow your own common sense and your gut feelings (even if courage is required). Thus, whenever your common sense and your gut feelings contradict what I have said, follow your own approach. You will recognize that suddenly it is easy to dive into the deep of large projects.

REFERENCES

Articles

Carmel, Erran, and Ritu Agarwal. "Tactical Approaches for Alleviating Distance in Global Software Development." *IEEE Software,* Vol. 18, No. 2 (March/April, 2001), pp. 22–29.

Cohn, Mike, and Doris Ford. "Introducing an Agile Process into an Organization." *IEEE Computer,* Vol. 36, No. 6 (June 2003), pp. 74–78.

Conway, Melvin E. "How Do Committees Invent?" *Datamation,* Vol. 14, No. 4 (April 1968), pp. 28–31.

Demmer, Christine. "Guetesiegel fuer fleissiges Aufschreiben" ("Mark of Quality for Busy Documenting"). *Sueddeutsche Zeitung, Bildung und Beruf,* No. 40, 16/17 (February 2002), p. V1/15.

Glazer, Hillel. "Dispelling the Process Myth: Having a Process Does Not Mean Sacrificing Agility or Creativity." *Crosstalk* (November 2001), pp. 27–30.

Jeffries, Ron. "Extreme Programming and the Capability Maturity Model." *XP Magazine,* http://www.xprogramming.com/xpmag/xpandcmm.htm (2000).

McConnell, Steve. "Best Practices: Daily Build and Smoke Test." *IEEE Software*, Vol. 13, No. 4 (July 1996), pp. 143–44.

Paulk, Mark C. "Extreme Programming from a CMM Perspective." *IEEE Software*, Vol. 18, No. 6 (Nov./Dec. 2001), pp. 19–26.

Salter, Chuck. "Attention Class!!! 16 Ways to Be a Smarter Teacher." *Fast Company*, Issue 53 (December 2001), p. 114.

van der Helm, Peer, and Dieter Stopper. "Von Makrelen und Menschen" ("About Mackerels and Human Beings"). *DAV Panorama*, No. 1, Issue 54 (2002), pp. 51–52.

Books

Ambler, Scott. *Agile Modeling: Effective Practices for Extreme Programming & the Unified Process.* New York: John Wiley & Sons, 2002.

Beck, Kent. *Extreme Programming Explained: Embrace Change.* Reading, Mass.: Addison-Wesley, 2000.

———, and Martin Fowler. *Planning Extreme Programming.* Reading, Mass.: Addison-Wesley, 2001.

Beckhard, Richard, and Wendy Pritchard. *Changing the Essence: The Art of Creating and Leading Fundamental Change in Organizations.* New York: John Wiley & Sons, 1992.

Brooks, Frederick P., Jr. *The Mythical Man-Month: Essays on Software Engineering,* 20th anniv. ed. Reading, Mass.: Addison-Wesley, 1995.

Cockburn, Alistair. *Agile Software Development.* Reading, Mass.: Addison-Wesley, 2002.

———. *Surviving Object-Oriented Projects.* Reading, Mass.: Addison-Wesley, 2001.

Cooper, Alan. *The Inmates Are Running the Asylum: Why High-Tech Products Drive Us Crazy and How to Restore the Sanity.* Indianapolis: Sams, 1999.

de Geus, Arie. *The Living Company: Habits for Survival in a Turbulent Business Environment.* Boston: Harvard Business School Press, 1997.

DeGrace, Peter, and Leslie Hulet Stahl. *Wicked Problems, Righteous Solutions: A Catalogue of Modern Software Engineering Paradigms.* Englewood Cliffs, N.J.: Prentice Hall, 1990.

DeMarco, Tom. *The Deadline: A Novel About Project Management.* New York: Dorset House Publishing, 1997.

————. *Slack: Getting Past Burnout, Busywork, and the Myth of Total Efficiency.* New York: Broadway Books, 2001.

————, and Timothy Lister. *Peopleware: Productive Projects and Teams,* 2nd ed. New York: Dorset House Publishing, 1999.

Fowler, Martin. *Refactoring: Improving the Design of Existing Code.* Reading, Mass.: Addison-Wesley, 1999.

Highsmith, James A., III. *Adaptive Software Development: A Collaborative Approach to Managing Complex Systems.* New York: Dorset House Publishing, 2000.

Hunt, Andrew, and David Thomas. *The Pragmatic Programmer: From Journeyman to Master.* Reading, Mass.: Addison-Wesley, 2000.

Kerth, Norman L. *Project Retrospectives: A Handbook for Team Reviews.* New York: Dorset House Publishing, 2001.

Larman, Craig. *Applying UML and Patterns: An Introduction to Object-Oriented Analysis and Design.* Englewood Cliffs, N.J.: Prentice Hall, 1998.

Leuf, Bo, and Ward Cunningham. *The Wiki Way: Collaboration and Sharing on the Internet.* Reading, Mass.: Addison-Wesley, 2001.

Manns, Mary Lynn, and Linda Rising. *Fear Less: Patterns for Introducing New Ideas into Organizations.* Boston: Addison-Wesley, 2004.

McBreen, Pete. *Software Craftsmanship: The New Imperative.* Reading, Mass.: Addison-Wesley, 2002.

Rechtin, Eberhardt, and Mark Maier. *The Art of Systems Architecting.* London: CRC Press, 2000.

Satir, Virginia, John Banmen, Jane Gerber, and Maria Gomori. *The Satir Model: Family Therapy and Beyond.* Palo Alto, Calif.: Science and Behavior Books, 1991.

Senge, Peter. *The Fifth Discipline: The Art & Practice of the Learning Organization.* New York: Currency Doubleday, 1998.

Sollmann, Ulrich, and Roderich Heinze. *Visionsmanagement: Erfolg als vorausgedachtes Ergebnis (Vision Management: Success As the Predefined Result).* Zürich: Orell Füssli, 1994.

Yourdon, Edward. *Death March: The Complete Software Developer's Guide to Surviving "Mission Impossible" Projects,* 2nd ed. Englewood Cliffs, N.J.: Prentice Hall, 2004.

URLs

Adaptive Software Development
http://www.adaptivesd.com/

Agile Manifesto
http://www.agilealliance.org/

Almost Extreme Programming
http://c2.com/cgi/wiki?AlmostExtremeProgramming/

ANT
http://www.ant.org/

Chrysler Comprehensive Compensation
http://c2.com/cgi/wiki?ChryslerComprehensiveCompensation/

Conway's Law
http://c2.com/cgi/wiki?ConwaysLaw/

CruiseControl
http://cruisecontrol.sourceforge.net/

Crystal Methodologies
http://alistair.cockburn.us/crystal/crystal.html

CVS
http://www.cvshome.org/

EasyMock
http://www.easymock.org/

Eclipse
http://www.eclipse.org/

Extreme Programming
http://c2.com/cgi/wiki?ExtremeProgrammingRoadmap/

Extreme Programming as a Trouble Detector
http://c2.com/cgi/wiki?ExtremeProgrammingAsTroubleDetector/

Feature Driven Development
http://www.featuredrivendevelopment.com/

Fit
http://fit.c2.com/

Gold Card
http://www.frankwestphal.de/xp2001/TimMackinnon.html

IntegrationGuard
http://iguard.sourceforge.net/

Jakarta
http://jakarta.apache.org/

JUnit
http://www.junit.org/

MockObjects
http://www.mockobjects.com/

Open Space
http://www.openspaceworld.org/

Optional Scope
http://groups.yahoo.com/group/extremeprogramming/files/
Optional%20scope%20contracts.pdf

Refactoring Tools
http://www.refactoring.com/tools.html

Scrum
http://www.controlchaos.com/

WebTest
http://webtest.canoo.com/

Wiki-Test
http://c2.com/cgi/wiki?TestingFramework/

XPlanner
http://www.xplanner.org/

XpPlanIt
http://xpplanit.canoo.com/

XP Software
http://www.xprogramming.com/software.htm

INDEX

Project Retrospectives
A Handbook for Team Reviews

by Norman L. Kerth
foreword by Gerald M. Weinberg

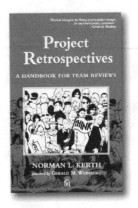

ISBN: 0-932633-44-7 ©2001 288 pages softcover
$39.95 (includes $6.00 for UPS in US)*

Use Team-Based Review Sessions to Maximize What You Learn from Each Project

With detailed scenarios, imaginative illustrations, and step-by-step instructions, consultant and speaker Norman L. Kerth guides readers through productive, empowering retrospectives of project performance.

Whether your shop calls them *postmortems* or *postpartums* or something else, project retrospectives offer organizations a formal method for preserving the valuable lessons learned from the successes and failures of every project. These lessons and the changes identified by the community will foster stronger teams and savings on subsequent efforts.

For a retrospective to be effective and successful, though, it needs to be safe. Kerth shows facilitators and participants how to defeat the fear of retribution and establish an air of mutual trust. One tool is Kerth's Prime Directive:

Regardless of what we discover, we must understand and truly believe that everyone did the best job he or she could, given what was known at the time, his or her skills and abilities, the resources available, and the situation at hand.

Applying years of experience as a project retrospective facilitator for software organizations, Kerth reveals his secrets for managing the sensitive, often emotionally charged issues that arise as teams relive and learn from each project.

Don't move on to your next project without consulting and using this readable, practical handbook. Each member of your team will be better prepared for the next deadline.

"This is one of the best written, best edited, most nicely presented, and most useful software books I've ever read.

"His sensitivity to the complex interpersonal issues surrounding project retrospectives will help any facilitator, participant, or manager get the most out of these important learning activities."
—**Karl Wiegers**, Process Impact
Author of *Creating a Software Engineering Culture*

"This is a book to read cover to cover and then use as a resource, project by project. It is a book for every process improvement coordinator, project leader, software manager, and consultant wishing to improve their organization's performance in learning from experience."
—**Carol A. Long**, *IEEE Software*

". . . a strong book, full of strong features . . . the classic work in this area."
—**Gerald M. Weinberg**, *from the Foreword*

Read more about Project Retrospectives *at www.dorsethouse.com/books/pr.html*

Order Today! • (800) 342-6657 • (212) 620-4053 • fax (212) 727-1044
Phone, fax, or mail with credit card information, check, or money order. *Prices subject to change without notice.
DORSET HOUSE PUBLISHING 353 WEST 12TH STREET NEW YORK, NEW YORK 10014 USA
info@dorsethouse.com • www.dorsethouse.com

Adaptive Software Development

A Collaborative Approach to Managing Complex Systems

by James A. Highsmith III

foreword by Ken Orr

ISBN: 0-932633-40-4   ©2000   392 pages   softcover
$50.95 (includes $6.00 for UPS in US)*

Winner of the Software Development Jolt Product Excellence Award

This innovative text offers a practical, realistic approach to managing high-speed, high-change software development projects. Consultant James A. Highsmith shows readers how to increase collaboration and adapt to uncertainty.

Many organizations start high-speed, high-change projects without knowing how to do them—and even worse, *without knowing they don't know.* Successful completion of these projects is often at the expense of the project team.

This book emphasizes an adaptive, collaborative approach to software development. The concepts allow developers to "scale-up" rapid application development and extreme programming approaches for use on larger, more complex projects.

The four goals of the book are to

- support an **adaptive culture** or mindset, in which change and uncertainty are assumed to be the natural state—not a false expectation of order

- introduce **frameworks** to guide the iterative process of managing change

- institute **collaboration**, the interaction of people on three levels: interpersonal, cultural, and structural

- add **rigor** and discipline to the RAD approach, making it scalable to the uncertainty and complexity of real-life undertakings

---

Read more about ADAPTIVE SOFTWARE DEVELOPMENT *at www.dorsethouse.com/books/asd.html*

Order Today! • (800) 342-6657 • (212) 620-4053 • fax (212) 727-1044
Phone, fax, or mail with credit card information, check, or money order. *Prices subject to change without notice.
DORSET HOUSE PUBLISHING 353 WEST 12TH STREET NEW YORK, NEW YORK 10014 USA
info@dorsethouse.com • www.dorsethouse.com